ENDORSE~~ME~~

Ephesians 6:12 tells us, *"...our fight is not against flesh and blood...."* A conscientious leader will not send his troops into battle without adequate preparation. We know that God, our commander in chief, has provided us with divine strategies and mighty weapons in order to prevail against every onslaught of the enemy.

In his book *Armed for Victory,* my friend pastor, Alan DiDio, will educate and equip you in the weapons of prayer found in the armory of God, and he will instruct you how to effectively use them to triumph in every spiritual battle.

DR. ROD PARSLEY
Pastor and Founder
World Harvest Church
Columbus, Ohio

I am convinced nothing changes outside of prayer. In his new book, *Armed for Victory,* my friend Alan DiDio gives not only a clarion call to what should be our first commitment, but also wisdom and strategy to function in that call. Anyone serious about leaving a lasting mark on their generation should devour this book.

ROBERT HENDERSON
Best-Selling Author of *Court of Heaven* Series

We have entered a new era and season for the church world-wide. This book, *Armed for Victory,* is a compelling and strategic writing for a strategic time. The history of nations hinges on the revelation contained within these pages. Alan has done a master-ful job of creating detailed imagery of natural wars and paralleling them with spiritual warfare. From preparation in warfare, dealing with the fear factor to a spiritual militancy that desperately needs to return to the church, you hold in your hands a download of insight from Heaven to navigate the end- time warfare. Alan directly challenges inward issues to bring about the most effective outward results. You will be enlightened and equipped in prayer and spiritual advancement; you will be *Armed for Victory* as you read. Thank you, Alan, for writing this timely and needed book!

KIM OWENS, Revivalist
Author, *Doorkeepers of Revival*
Pastor, Fresh Start Church, Peoria, AZ

In *Armed for Victory,* Alan DiDio delivers a message that will mobilize the end-times remnant church and equip them with the heavenly weapons and strategies they need to be victorious in these last days.

SHAUN TABATT
Co-Author of *Real Near Death Experience Stories*

You know when you hold a book in your hand and the message within the pages announces loudly, "FOR SUCH A TIME AS THIS!" This incredible book by my friend, Alan DiDio, is just that. This book is a gift from the Holy Spirit to the church right now. It is a treasure chest of wisdom and revelation for the day and era we are in. It is a weapon that the Lord has given to the church through Alan and it is a loud divine reminder of the victory we have in Christ. This book will arm you with insight, revelation, and biblical truth. You will be armed with the Word of God to move and grow further into your authority in Christ.

He is raising up warriors who are ferociously focused on Jesus, not ignorant of the devil's schemes, and will burn with the fire of the victory and authority of Jesus and the name above every other name. Get ready for revelation from the Holy Spirit that will prepare you for the days ahead.

LANA VAWSER

Author of *The Prophetic Voice of God, A Time to Selah,* and *I Hear the Lord Say "New Era"*

Lana Vawser Ministries

Neville Chamberlain made peace with Hitler and declared, "We will have peace in our time!" You don't make peace with the devil. The West slept while Germany rearmed and warred. Then Churchill mobilized the English language and sent it into war and armed England for victory! Now, in another hour of rising earthly tyrants threatening World War and the ascendancy of demonic powers boasting their dominion of deception and death over the hopeless and hapless billions of the earth, my revival friend Alan DiDio has written a book that has mobilized the words of the Bible and sent them into war. It shatters the spiritual pacifism of the church, sends her into war, and hands out spiritual weapons to every citizen of the Kingdom. No more will it be said, "They are building bombs, we are building refrigerators," as in the days of Pearl Harbor. The book summons us into and trains us for the cosmic battle we have been thrust into at the end of the age. The book has shaken me. It will shake you! It will give the Lion back its roar. Churchill time! The Church on a Hill!

LOU ENGLE

Author of *Digging The Wells of Revival*

Brother Alan DiDio has crafted a strategic plan for every church and every believer to take on hell with a water pistol and win in these crucial last days. Armed for Victory makes it clear: The days of the cruise ship church of potlucks and endless Bible studies are over. We must expose and engage in a very real war taking place in both the natural and supernatural realm. Read this book and get on board the battleship the church is meant to be as Alan provides bullets for your prophetic pistol to shoot down the enemy's schemes and terminate his tactics. Comprehensive, powerful and prophetic. This book will show you how to go behind enemy lines and rescue POWs from the gates of hell itself. Thank you, Pastor Alan, for firing this book as a warning shot to the church and the devil himself. WE WIN!

TROY BREWER
Author of *Redeeming Your Timeline*
Senior Pastor OpenDoor Church, Burleson, TX

Alan DiDio is a refreshing voice in this generation who is trailblazing a path forward for the end-time church. In this precious book, you will be challenged to take the moral high ground and empowered in the fight for it. I pray God will use Alan's words to light a fire in complacent hearts and also give language to those embracing present day awakening and revival.

JEREMIAH JOHNSON
Founder of The Altar Global and Best-Selling Author

A call of the Spirit. This is what you will hear in Alan Didio's message. He is not just another voice, but one echoing the calling of God from His heart to ours.

From the moment I first heard Alan, I recognized in his unique presentation an equally unique anointing designated for this hour in time. You will find no parroting here; the words of this book come from a deep understanding of the ways of God from someone who has spent time in His presence. He has been in the planning room and heard divine intelligence.

As someone who has been concerned about the body of Christ being stuck in "boot camp" and not prepared for what is coming, I am thrilled this book is being released. No one can say this like Alan can. Cutting out all religious and political distractions, he distills the message down to its pure essence. Clearly and precisely, he outlines what the church of Jesus Christ needs to know and DO right now.

READ THIS BOOK!

ANNETTE CAPPS
Author of *Quantum Faith* and *The Spirit of Prophecy*
President of Capps Ministries

ARMED FOR
VICTORY

PRAYER STRATEGIES THAT UNLOCK
THE END-TIME ARMORY OF GOD

ALAN DIDIO

DESTINY IMAGE® PUBLISHERS, INC.
P.O. Box 310, Shippensburg, PA 17257-0310
"Promoting Inspired Lives."

This book and all other Destiny Image and Destiny Image Fiction books are available at Christian bookstores and distributors worldwide.

For more information on foreign distributors, call 717-532-3040.

Reach us on the Internet: www.destinyimage.com.

ISBN 13 TP: 978-0-7684-6168-8
ISBN 13 eBook: 978-0-7684-6169-5
ISBN 13 HC: 978-0-7684-6171-8
ISBN 13 LP: 978-0-7684-6170-1

For Worldwide Distribution, Printed in the U.S.A.

1 2 3 4 5 6 7 8 / 26 25 24 23 22

CONTENTS

FOREWORD

General George S. Patton said, "Untutored courage is useless in the face of educated bullets." Simply stated, no matter how gung ho a soldier is, unless he is properly trained he is dead meat before a seasoned enemy.

He could have just as easily been talking to the modern church. We have taken massive casualties in spiritual warfare because of arrogant, foolish, and false teaching. We are inundated by voices that jump on social media boasting of results against sickness and devils that are just plain false.

Satan laughs at our theatrics and our theories. Spiritual shenanigans have made the prophetic pathetic and the supernatural superficial.

Nevertheless, we should not let go of God's promises! We must hold fast the promise that the "weapons of our warfare are not carnal but mighty to the tearing down of strongholds" (2 Cor. 10:4).

In the book *Armed for Victory* by Pastor Alan DiDio, you will experience an exciting, powerful, and effective battle plan. The Holy Spirit will use this book in conjunction with the Bible to turn you into an "educated bullet"! You will see why we have failed. You will gain true authority over evil. You will understand the modern enemy. You will unlock the mighty revelation of how God is preparing us for a final glorious worldwide offensive for souls and reformation.

—MARIO MURILLO

CHAPTER ONE

HEARING THE VOICE OF SATAN

I still shudder when I recall that evening—not because the weather was chilly, but because of the terror that I felt in my soul. I had just come face to face with the fact that I was entrenched in a battle I had not even known existed, and I was being held captive by an enemy I had not even believed existed.

I was sitting in the back of a multi-purpose room at a friend's church. The music was blaring as teens played foosball, ate pizza, and hung out. You can imagine the steady roar that comes from a large room full of young people. Everyone was having a wonderful time—except me.

I was sitting there trying to collect my thoughts when, all of a sudden, I felt like I was being sucked into a tunnel. All the raucous sound around me became muted as if I were underwater. When I looked up, I could see everyone's mouths moving, but I could not hear the words they were saying. Everything was muffled, except for the sound of one voice.

This singular voice was audible and hideous. The grotesque and bone-chilling nature of the voice gave itself away. I knew immediately that this was the voice of the devil—and that he was real.

"Christian Atheists"

As a young man reared in the buckle of the Bible Belt, I had seen the hypocrisy of churchgoers as they sat in judgment over others, completely blind to the beam in their own eye.

By the age of seventeen, I had convinced myself that I was an atheist. As ridiculous a conclusion as that was, I did not come to it on my own. As I mentioned in my book *Encounter*, I had the help of lots and lots of Christians. I like to call them "Christian atheists."

To me, a "Christian atheist" is someone who claims to believe in God but lives like He does not exist. Do you know anyone like that? These people may attend church and even read their Bibles, yet they are complete strangers to the God they claim to worship.

I often wondered, *If their God is real, why are they so depressed and bitter?* On the surface they looked good, but underneath all the stereotypes they were working so feverishly to maintain, they were empty. With no spiritual depth or scriptural foundation, their testimony spoke to an atheist—like me—as proof that God did not exist.

Here is a fact that I believe everyone knows instinctively in their hearts: if Christianity is not supernatural, it is superficial.

That is why people from all cultures and faiths recoil in disgust at the Christian hypocrite. Somehow, we can all agree that a Christian without power is a charlatan of the worst kind.

Satan uses this instinct as a sermon illustration in his manipulation of the masses—and it works. It is easy for him to distract us from our own need for repentance by having us point a finger at someone else.

If our spiritual reflection is directed at the perceived hypocrite, our focus will not be on our *own* need to consider Christ and His indisputable power for our lives.

It was a cold January evening, more than two decades ago, when I had this encounter that led me to the saving grace of Jesus Christ. Admittedly, my testimony is an unusual one, but God reaches all of us with exactly what we need. God's grace opened my ears (and my eyes) to a world of warfare that would transform my life forever. I had asked God to show me that He was real, and on this night, I would receive more than I bargained for.

Several days before my encounter, I was invited to a revival service. The evangelistic pestering of my friend ensued. After I repeatedly rejected his annoying invites, he played on my love for music and told me about a great choir that would be performing that night.

Hesitantly, I agreed to go—but with conditions. I insisted that we sit in the back so that I would be able to leave if I felt uncomfortable. He agreed, yet somehow that night, we ended up sitting in the second row.

I immediately discovered that this was a Pentecostal church. People were shouting "Hallelujah!" and speaking in some odd language that I had never heard before. I felt as though I had just walked into a cult compound, and I was not sure if I should fear for my life!

That may be a slight exaggeration, but to simply say I was "concerned" would be an understatement. Then, before I could locate an exit and plot my escape, people started receiving prayer and falling on the floor at the altar. You may be accustomed to this kind of behavior, but it can be scary for someone who has never witnessed it before.

A Prophecy from a Preacher

Suddenly, the preacher—who was far too loud and sweaty for my taste—pointed his finger at yours truly.

"Me?" I timidly looked over each shoulder hoping that his attention was directed at someone else. No such luck. The minister summoned me to the altar and prophesied these words over me:

> Just like the prophet Elisha laid on that Shunammite woman's son to bring him to life in the natural, this prophet is laying hands on you to bring you to life in the spirit. You will live and not die! I am going to make you an example of what I can do with a young man sold out to Me, says the Lord.

In that moment, I felt nothing but *anger* at my friend for subjecting me to this nonsense, and *disgust* for what I considered to be religious fraud. However, it was my hard shell of skepticism that was the real fraud.

Speaking as the pastor I now am, you cannot be moved by the way people react to your presentation of the gospel. Underneath their cynical exterior, there is a heart that is being assaulted by the powers of darkness. The same evil forces that were at work against me are at work against them. They are sometimes unable to receive at that moment in time because of the struggles they are undergoing in their own hearts.

When I left the service that night, something was happening *in* me that was greater than what had happened *to* me. Underneath my perceptions and preconceived ideas, God was preparing my heart for an encounter.

After what I thought of as a distressing experience, I swore that I would never darken the doors of that church again. Three days later, though, I was back. I justified this violation of my oath by the fact that I was not going to a church service. My friend had assured me that this was a party for teens with games, girls, and free food. Surely nothing weird would happen!

After that initial revival service, I had become increasingly troubled in my mind and had felt surrounded by a darkness that was exhausting. I do not remember much about the three days that passed or what exactly brought me back to this church, but I do remember that darkness hanging over me like a turbulent, tormenting cloud.

My mind raced with thoughts like, *You don't believe in any of this! God is not real! Christianity is a crutch for the weak-minded! Stay away from those people!*

An Encounter and a Revelation

As I walked into the church the evening of the party, I was consumed with doubts. I could hardly hold my head up due to the weight of the conviction I was experiencing. It was with this mindset that I sought out a place to sit by myself in the back of the room. That was when I was drawn into the soundless tunnel and heard the voice of satan.

Up until that moment, I had assumed that I was the one who was in control of my thoughts. In an instant, God showed me that there were spiritual entities influencing the direction of my life by deceptively manipulating my thoughts.

The evil voice I heard was repeating the very same thoughts that had been bombarding my mind for the last three days: *"You don't believe in God! Get out of here! Get away from these people!"* It was as though God had pulled back the curtain—like on *The Wizard of Oz*—and let me hear who was really doing the talking in my own mind.

But here is the glorious miracle of it all: the frightening nature of this audible voice was immediately neutralized by the grace of God, which allowed me to hear how desperate and weak the voice seemed. The devil was hanging on by a thread; there was nothing he could do if I chose to give my life to Jesus. I didn't know how to pray, so I just said, "Satan, you can't have me anymore. Jesus, I'm all Yours."

As quickly as this encounter came, it left. The room went back to normal, and I could hear everyone once again. I began to weep uncontrollably. People started to gather around me to see if I was okay. I felt compelled to have them turn off the music and gather around so that I could share what had just happened to me. I did not yet know that Romans 10:10 says, *"For with the heart man believeth unto righteousness; and with the mouth confession is made unto salvation."*

The instant I shared my newfound faith, the darkness lifted, the torment ceased, and the weights I did not know I was carrying were taken off my shoulders. *I was a new creature.*

In one brief moment, I had encountered both the presence of satan and the presence of God—and God won! That is why we call our ministry *Encounter Today.* I want others to have the same encounter with Christ's revealing and delivering power.

This was not simply a revelation of satan in the life of an atheist. This was a revelation of spiritual warfare. How long had these unseen forces been manipulating me? How could I be assured that I would never yield to them again?

For years, I had been bound by thoughts that I assumed were my own. Now, I knew differently. The reality is that the enemy of our souls often operates with impunity as we go on with the delusion that our thoughts are always our own.

Through this book, I want to expose your enemy and arm you for victory. Here are some of the questions about this spiritual warfare for which the body of Christ desperately needs answers:

- What is the true nature of this war?

- How does this struggle affect individuals—and nations?

- What does the enemy look like in the 21st century?

- What weapons has God given us to fight this spiritual battle?

- Are there universal warfare strategies that can assure victory?

- Can we ignore or misuse God's weapons at our own peril?

In this book, I will seek to answer these questions and more, trusting it will help prepare you and the church for victory over the forces of the darkness of this age. I have searched the scriptures, studied under generals, traveled the world, and worked with the underground church. I have discovered that this war is not limited to the fringes of the charismatic movement; it is ubiquitous to the human experience.

Every human being, whether saved or lost, is entrenched in an invisible war, the stakes of which are eternal. The first and most important issue is: *"Have you given the whole of your life to Jesus Christ?"*

Do not allow the enemy to pull the wool over your eyes and dominate your thought life like he did mine. Fear, depression, anxiety, addiction, and condemnation can all be banished from your life if you will forsake your sin, repent, and give everything to the one who gave it all for you.

If you want real and lasting victory, you need to make Jesus the general of your life. You can start by simply praying the same prayer that I prayed those many years ago: *"Satan, you can't have me anymore! Jesus, I'm all Yours!"*

The Joshua Generation

This book was not written to *entertain* you; it was written to *train* you. We have too many preachers and teachers whose entire goal is to outdo themselves each week by dishing out some new and fresh inspirational speech that tickles ears more than it crucifies flesh. This book is meant to draw a line in the sand and present you with a choice. The purpose of preaching is not to entertain or even to inspire, though it can do both. The primary purpose of the ministry of the Word of God is to get you to decide.

This war is a battle of obedience, and each side wants you to choose to obey them. Obedience is the doorway that gives spiritual forces access into this natural world. During your walk with Jesus, you will be faced with a myriad of decisions. Your choice will determine which kingdom can come into the earth.

The war is already raging; the choice is there, waiting to be made. We must consistently choose obedience to God and His Word if we wish to see consistent victory. Here is what the Bible says about making our choice:

> *But if it is unpleasing in your sight to serve the Lord, then choose for yourselves this day whom you will serve, whether the gods your fathers served beyond the Euphrates, or the gods of the Amorites in whose land you are living. As for me and my house, we will serve the Lord* (Joshua 24:15 BSB).

Many believers have one foot in the Kingdom of God and the other foot in the world. They have never really made the decision to follow God wholeheartedly, so when affliction and persecution arise for the Word's sake, they are offended and fall away. It is not *divine destiny* that determines your future. It is *your decisions* that determine your future. The victory has been secured, but it is only activated by those who "*choose life*" (Deut. 30:19). It is time for you to make a choice.

This war reaches farther than you might think. If you have not already made Jesus the Lord of your life, now is the time to repent and to trust in Him for your eternal salvation. If you are a Christian with hidden sins for which you have not repented, now is the time to get things right. This moment is too precious to spoil with the cares of this world or the lusts of other things. Take a moment right now to turn away from sin and receive forgiveness for anything that may be between your soul and your Savior. God is calling you to enlist.

Spiritual Cold War

For some time now, there has been a spiritual cold war brewing within the church. The battle lines have been drawn between the house of Saul and the house of David. During this time, the spiritually hot have been getting hotter and the spiritually cold have been getting colder. Can you feel it?

On one side, there is a creeping apathy that is trying to corrode your zeal and dull your passion; on the other side, there is a persistent hunger and a stirring in your heart for more of His presence. Which will you yield to?

This spiritual battle is not being drawn along denominational lines. I believe that in the coming days, we will find ourselves allied with the most unlikely candidates. This is a battle between those who are hungry for reformation and those who are satisfied with church as usual. There are individuals who believe that the church should influence culture, and there are others whose apathy will allow the culture to influence the church. There really is no middle ground—we must align ourselves with one side or the other. And once we do that, it will be time to choose a weapon.

A Burning Bush or a Gleaming Sword?

There are weapons, forged in the breath of God and tempered in the blood of His Son, that God wants to place in your hands.

When God was leading His people into the Promised Land, He used two incredibly similar leaders, Moses and Joshua. It is interesting to consider what these two men had in common:

- They both had a dramatic encounter with the divine.

- They both were commanded to remove their sandals because they were on holy ground.

- They both saw waters part (the Red Sea and the Jordan River).

- They both sent out spies.

- They both preached lengthy sermons just before their death.

However, what they had in common is not nearly as interesting as what was different about them:

- Moses led them out of bondage, while Joshua led them into the Promised Land.

- Moses parted the Red Sea to escape their enemies, while Joshua parted the Jordan to attack their enemies.

- Moses led them into deliverance, while Joshua led them into victory.

- Moses never made it into the Promised Land, while Joshua eventually took possession of it.

As we enter a new era of church history, it is important for us to understand that we are a part of a Joshua generation. Both Moses and Joshua were launched into their destiny with a divine encounter. Moses had a burning bush; Joshua had a gleaming sword.

I know that it may seem like the enemy has unlimited resources and unfettered access into our lives. However, as the Son of God was kicked and prodded down the cobblestone streets of Jerusalem 2,000 years ago, He was forging weapons. Jesus did not go to the cross to create *blinders* for us so we could ignore our enemy. Jesus suffered and rose from the dead to create *armor* with which we can overcome our enemy. He died so that you could wear His armor and wield the sword of the Spirit.

Moses was confronted with a burning bush, but Joshua encountered a gleaming sword.

And it came to pass, when Joshua was by Jericho, that he lifted up his eyes and looked, and, behold, there stood a man over against him with his sword drawn in his hand: and Joshua went unto him, and said unto him, Art thou for us, or for our adversaries? And he said, Nay; but as captain of the host of the Lord am I now come. And Joshua fell on his face to the earth, and did worship, and said unto him, What saith my Lord unto his servant? And the captain of the Lord's host said unto Joshua, Loose thy shoe from off thy foot; for the place whereon thou standest is holy. And Joshua did so (Joshua 5:13-15).

One of the characters created by the great playwright William Shakespeare said, "Some are born great, some achieve greatness, and some have greatness thrust upon 'em" (*Twelfth Night*, William Shakespeare, 1623).

Although many of us would have loved being born in a time when we could have had the beauty of a burning bush experience, God has more for this generation. Here is the good news: you were not only *born* for the battle, but you were *born again* to win the battle!

When picking the name of the Messiah, it is fascinating that God did not choose the name of the great deliverer, Moses. Instead, He chose the name of the great conqueror, Joshua (Yeshua/Jesus). It is the spirit of this conqueror that dwells on the inside of you.

This is the season of the sword of the Lord and of His church. You are going to learn to wield His name and His word in such a way that your enemies will not be able to contend with or run from it. This is a season of battle, and this is the season of your victory.

There is a great shaking taking place right now. God is about to exalt those who are His and expose those who are His enemies. The Lord Almighty is pouring out His Spirit and equipping those who are His with weapons that have not been seen for generations. Will you be prepared to wield God's end-time weaponry?

CHAPTER TWO

A WAR FOOTING

How are the mighty fallen, and the weapons of war perished!

—2 SAMUEL 1:27

"Any officer who goes into action without his sword is improperly dressed."

—COLONEL "MAD JACK" CHURCHILL[1]

The year was 1943, and World War II was well under way. This was a time of extraordinary technological advancement in conventional warfare. Germany had invested heavily in the development of new and improved weaponry like long-range missiles and guided weapons. With ordnance like these, it was becoming increasingly difficult to defeat them in battle and to keep up the morale of the allies.

As generals and military strategists scurried to find new ways to counter these innovative weapons, there was one man who took a different approach. His name was Jack Churchill. "Mad Jack," as he would later be called, was a British commando who preferred a more classic approach to warfare. When the ramps of the landing craft fell, he would be the first to leap out and run toward the enemy with a sword and a longbow. He sounds like a fictitious character out of a comic book, but his real-life story is stranger than fiction.

There were times when "Mad Jack" was seen charging toward the enemy, playing bagpipes and tossing grenades. He was a legend in his day, and nearly every enemy soldier on the front lines had nightmares about the British commando who hunted Nazis at night with the silent and artful precision of a longbow.

It is reported that Mad Jack once captured 42 armed soldiers at one time with nothing but his basket-hilted Scottish long sword. Think about that for a moment. The enemy, despite all the advances in warfare technology, feared—and lost to—one man with one weapon: a single sword!

The same thing holds true today. Although we have made great advancements in our understanding of spiritual warfare, there is truly nothing new under the sun (see Eccles. 1:9). When it comes to the battle between light and dark, good and evil, there is nothing more powerful and effective than the sword of the Spirit, which is the Word of God (see Eph. 6:17).

There are also some additional weapons in the arsenal of God that have not been seen for generations. I believe that the

Holy Spirit is about to place these weapons into our hands. Though they may appear to be new, do not be mistaken. They are tried and tested instruments for attack and defense in spiritual combat.

You are about to be trained in the art of doing battle in a spiritual war. In this book, you will discover strategies that the enemy has long hidden from the church because, if ever mastered, they mean the end of his demonic occupation in your life.

A War Footing

Here is a passage from *The Ephesian Mandate*, a manual of instruction I recently released on how to gird yourself with the armor of God in these last days. It speaks to the tenuous stance regarding spiritual warfare that much of the church has adopted today:

> In the last 3,400 years, the earth has only known 268 years of peace. Only eight percent of the last three millenniums have been war free. At the writing of this book, there are thirty wars going on around the world. There are few things more common to the human experience than battle.
>
> Even in times of peace, nations plan for war and soldiers are trained for war because we understand the inevitability of war. I can remember, as I'm sure many of us do, the morning of September 11, 2001, as terrorists turned three passenger planes into guided missiles. Over 2,500 United States citizens died on that day, as our nation searched

for answers. How could this happen? How could a handful of backwater radicals perpetrate such a strike on American soil? After all the intel was examined and the commissions were completed, we had our answer: They were at war with us, but we were not at war with them.

America was not on a war footing against radical Islam. As a result, the enemy was able to slip in unawares. Throughout history, we have learned that we are most at risk as a nation when we are war weary. The church faces a similar challenge today. Surrounded by enemies on every side, the average Christian goes about their day, casually quoting scripture and carelessly praying prayers without passion or meaning. As a result, the Church is assailed and assaulted with unexpected, yet pre-dictable, blows.[2]

The New Testament is replete with references to the spiritual war in which we are all engaged. Jesus spoke more about casting out devils than He did about Heaven. Why? Because He understood that from the moment we are born again, we are born into a battle. His life and ministry were perfect illustrations of this.

From the moment Jesus was baptized, He was engaged in hand-to-hand spiritual combat with the enemy (see Matt. 4). He was ready and prepared when the enemy came to challenge Him, and He wants to make us ready for when the enemy will inevitably come to challenge us as well.

We cannot choose whether or not we will be in a battle. That choice was made when we were *born*, and again when we were *born again*. The choice we have to make is whether or not we will participate in the victory Christ has already won.

Situational Awareness

Before we dive into the different weapons God has ready and waiting for us, we need a revival of situational awareness. Self-defense guru Jeff Cooper lays out what I am talking about in his book *Principles of Personal Defense*. This former firearms instructor and Marine makes such a strong case for situational awareness that his teachings are still used in many military colleges today. He contests that when going into battle, it is not your weapon or your combat skills that will ultimately save you—it is your situational awareness. If you are unaware, you are unprepared. Technically speaking, situational awareness is the use of your senses to identify threats around you and to predict them in the future.

Tourists in big cities can become easily recognizable targets to criminals because they are so enamored with their environment that they are unaware of their surroundings. Something as simple as having all your attention on your cell phone as you walk down the street can make you a target. The enemy looks for those who are unaware. Warfare awareness is what is needed today in the church.[3]

Your success in warfare prayer hinges on this kind of vigilance. It can change everything! Imagine for a moment that you are going about your day and preforming tasks that require very little thought. Whether it is walking into the grocery store or going to get your mail, these things can be done while sipping on a latte and scrolling through your phone (and they often are). So much of what we do in our natural and spiritual lives is like these tasks. From getting ready for church on Sunday to praying over our meals, very little energy is expended in performing these duties.

Let's take one scenario as an example of how warfare awareness can change everything. Imagine you are going to pick up something at the grocery store. Simple enough? Now, envision that there have been six armed robberies in that very parking lot in the last week. This would certainly change the way you picture yourself going about this rudimentary task. You would no longer stroll casually through the parking lot. Your awareness would be heightened, your head would be on a swivel, and you might even have your car keys protruding through your tightly clenched fist, just in case!

If you knew that armed thugs were frequenting your favorite grocery store parking lot, you could do one of several things:

- Arm yourself
- Take reinforcements with you
- Avoid high-risk scenarios (such as going after dark, not noticing your surroundings)
- Avoid the place entirely

In the midst of conflict, your attention to detail is *elevated* while every step is *calculated*. This is warfare awareness, and every Christian needs a heaping double dose of it. This will change how we approach prayer. And when we understand the true nature of the conflict, it will alter how we prepare for church, how we give our offerings, and even how we pray over our food. We're in a battle, and the sooner we realize that fact, the sooner we'll find God's grace to fight it—and win!

I've heard it said, and it bears repeating, that before the church can have a *great* awakening it needs a *rude* awakening. What is it that we need to be awakened *to?* We need to become aware that we are already in a battle.

Jesus revealed that it was only *"while men slept"* that the enemy could come in and sow tares among the wheat (Matt. 13:25). An unaware church is an unarmed church. Are you aware that you have a spiritual foe who is endeavoring to thwart everything you attempt for the Kingdom?

What does or should *warfare awareness* look like in your life? Paul said to the church at Ephesus that after his departure *"grievous wolves"* would arise from among them (the leaders at Ephesus) and would not spare the flock (Acts 20:29).

Obviously, someone was not paying attention. Attention to detail can mean the difference between success and failure, between victory and disaster. The New Testament is constantly warning us to watch and to be sober (see 1 Pet. 5:8). Are we?

Unaware = Unarmed

Think of it this way: we are in the middle of a fight that has already been won. What is required of us is alertness. It is my belief that if we can awaken our awareness, we will awaken much of the armory of God.

*There was no smith found throughout all the land
of Israel: for the Philistines said, Lest the Hebrews
make them swords* (1 Samuel 13:19).

At this time in history, the Philistines had taken away all the blacksmiths so that God's people could not make swords for their army. They had defeated the Philistines twenty years earlier, and yet, somehow, under Samuel's leadership they had lost their weapons. They even had to visit the enemy's camp if they wanted their farming tools sharpened!

Today, the enemy has managed, little by little, to creep into the church and remove our weapons. We've lost our edge. Now churches run to secular leadership gurus to sharpen their church growth tools.

We have become unarmed in the American church, and I'm not talking about the Second Amendment. The church is no longer clothed with the breastplate of righteousness—we have to go to the Philistines to see what's right or acceptable. We no longer have the loin belt of truth; we have to go to the tech monopolies so that they can tell us what's true.

The same was true during the reign of the wicked queen Athaliah (see 2 Kings 11). This daughter of Jezebel had managed to kill all the righteous seed who could challenge her reign—or so she thought. As Athaliah began her reign of terror, a priest's wife stole a young baby away and hid him in the house of God. The house of God is a good place to hide until you come to maturity.

The young baby was Joash, who would become the eighth king of Judah. When the child turned seven years old, it was time to challenge Athaliah's power and install him as king, but they didn't have any weapons! Like the Philistines, Athaliah had made it impossible for those loyal to the true king to have access to weapons. What she didn't know was that there were still some old weapons left in the house of God:

> *And to the captains over hundreds did the priest give king David's spears and shields, that were in the temple of the Lord* (2 Kings 11:10).

There were still some weapons capable of overthrowing the devil's kingdom, but they were hidden in the house of God. I wonder what kind of demonic occupation we're tolerating today because of our own ignorance concerning God's end-time weapons. This isn't the only time that we see weapons hidden in the house of God.

The House of the Forest

The Bible speaks of a mysterious place called the House of the Forest (see Isa. 22:8). In a season of war, when Hezekiah was facing certain doom from the Assyrians, the Bible says that he looked to "*the armor of the house of the forest.*"

At the time, Hezekiah looked in vain because he was not looking to the Lord, but what was it that gave him such hope in the face of certain death? It was an armory full of unmatched military hardware. This armory, also called the House of the Forest of Lebanon (1 Kings 7:2), had been specifically designed by King Solomon to contain his choicest weapons.

This building was 83 feet longer than the Temple that Solomon built and 62 feet wider. It had 15 rows of cedar pillars that were 4 rows deep.

> *And king Solomon made two hundred targets of beaten gold: six hundred shekels of gold went to one target. And he made three hundred shields of beaten gold; three pound of gold went to one shield: and the king put them in the house of the forest of Lebanon* (1 Kings 10:16-17).

The "*targets of beaten gold*" mentioned here were like miniature breastplates that protected the neck and heart. Today, each one would be worth about $1.5 million.

The "*shields of beaten gold*" would have been worth nearly $900,000 today. The cost of these weapons should come as no surprise—the temple itself had an estimated worth of $174 billion. These were weapons unlike anything seen before or since, and their spiritual equivalents are still available today!

There are so many battles that weary believers and leave them defeated simply because they did not know how to utilize the right weapons for the job. God is about to change that. He is awakening His armor, even now, as our warfare awareness is revived.

Overcome Fear: Awaken the Armor

Fear and intimidation give way to compromise and manipulation. In order to awaken the armor of God, we must eliminate fear from our lives. The fear-wracked soul is too preoccupied with its present distress to hear truth, even if it comes from someone who loves them. Fear immobilizes; faith has movement.

The hideousness of fear and its blatant objectives make it easy to rouse a people who desire to move from where they are to where God has called them to be. When we can see our enemy clearly and are sensitive to the discomfort of our bondage, we long for freedom. But, like the frog in the kettle, what happens when we become accustomed to captivity?

Many people have become so captivated by fear that they don't even recognize their need to be free from it.

Here's a question that every soul-winning evangelical needs to ponder: how do we communicate fear's insidiousness to a people who *want* to remain bound and immobilized by it? There is a certain level of comfort that comes with captivity. Would we rather be entertained than engaged in a battle for freedom?

We live in a society of people who long, not for freedom, but for comfort and unconsciousness. Sadly, this is also true for the church, and it explains the success of many modern mega-ministries. Conservative commentator and Jewish theologian Dennis Prager, in a speech to high school students in Washington D.C., said:

> The human being responds naturally to leftism, not Americanism. Leftism is more natural. It says the state will take care of you. More people are interested in being taken care of than in being free. Liberty is not a universal yearning. Liberty is

a value. ...People think everyone wants to be free.
If everyone wanted to be free, then there would be
a lot of United States of Americas around. They
don't. They yearn to be taken care of. Americans
yearned to be free.[4]

Politics aside, this statement accurately describes our hidden
inner longings. Liberty is not the natural state of fallen men,
and the success of a consumer-based civilization is predicated
on man's desire to unplug and be cared for. The American culture today speaks to our baser instincts of fear, lust, or anger,
and sells us knee-jerk reactions.

We are not asked to think, or to consider, or to be in the moment.
We are asked to respond to the tantalization of our viler senses. I
often wonder if today's fascination with zombies is our own subcon-
scious awareness of this mindless state in which we find ourselves.

The church is sleepwalking. We've been lulled into a sleep
that goes undetected because we're still able to move around.
However, that means our movements are all instinctual instead
of thoughtful. Why do we allow this? The simple answer: fear.
We're afraid of making a mistake. We are afraid of not being
loved. We're afraid of failing. We're afraid of being taken advantage of, and the list goes on and on.

The pressure can become so overwhelming that we will take
any and every opportunity to turn off or shut down and forget
about the failures of our past or the impending responsibilities
of our future. We need an awakening!

Cowardice keeps us asleep (or at least in bed with the covers
over our heads). This is why Christianity is perceived as being

difficult. We have a natural aversion to true religion because *it demands an awakening.* The Cross demands that we take a long, awkward glance in the mirror and then prophesies that we won't like what we see. William Gurnall, a 17th century English writer and clergyman, said, *"It requires more prowess and greatness of spirit to obey God faithfully than to command an army of men; more greatness to be a Christian than a captain."*[5]

Christianity is at war with the world around us as well as with the world within us. In order to win, the first casualty has to be ourselves (see Gal. 2:20). If you want to be armed for victory, the first casualty has to be you. The carnal Christian, without warfare awareness, is asleep to the dangers of his sinful state. Like Samson we're not taken captive by the Philistines, but by the hidden sins of our own hearts. The Philistines are just there to reap the benefits of our carnality. This is why the Christian must be armed with the weapons from *"the House of the Forest of Lebanon."*

Spiritual Stockholm Syndrome

In 1973, there was a bank robbery in Stockholm, Sweden, where many hostages were taken. After the ordeal was over, the hostages refused to testify against their captors. They had developed an affinity with those who had threatened to steal, kill, and destroy. Though rare, this condition is now referred to as "Stockholm Syndrome." It refers to an unnatural bond and affection some hostages develop for their abductors. This is a difficult question, but I want you to prayerfully consider it: "Am I addicted to my captivity? Do I have an affection for those things that are controlling me?"

Unfortunately, most of us have no enmity with the world around us today. We aren't at odds with our culture anymore. Perhaps this is why the youth of this generation have so little interest in our services. They are looking for a fight, so they turn away from a pacifist church to embrace the camaraderie of the foxhole.

Some find their place in false religions, but more find it in false beliefs. Today's political parties often become a dangerous substitute for the divine, with their moral grandstanding and pompous leaders. Christianity demands love and virtue, but the platforms of these parties have no moral compass. They create an atmosphere where near-religious devotees can give an excuse for anything, so long as the end justifies the means. It's time to give this generation something to fight for—or against.

God will not open His armory for the fearful. Take a moment to repent of all fear, insecurity, anxiety, or lack of trust. Receive the grace of God by faith, and get ready to wake up and live a life of bold vulnerability and daring victory.

Notes

1. Katie Serena, "World War II's Biggest Badass Killed a Nazi with a Longbow, among Other Awesome Feats," All That's Interesting, October 26, 2021, https://allthatsinteresting.com/mad-jack-churchill.

2. Alan Didio, *The Ephesian Mandate* (2021).

3. Jeff Cooper, *Principles of Personal Defense* (Boulder, CO: Paladin Press, 2006).

4. Robert Kraychik, "Dennis Prager: Leftists 'Don't Believe in National Identities,'" Breitbart, July 25, 2018, https://www.breitbart.com/the-media/2018/07/24/dennis-prager-leftists-dont-believe-in-national-identities.

5. William Gurnall, essay in *The Christian in Compleat Armour: Or, a Treatise of the Saints War Against the Devil [...] the First Part* (London: Printed for Ralph Smith, 1656), 9.

CHAPTER THREE

PROPHETIC INTELLIGENCE BRIEFING

By faith Rahab the prostitute did not perish with those who were disobedient, because she had given a friendly welcome to the spies.

—HEBREWS 11:31 ESV

"In preparing for battle I have always found that plans are useless, but planning is indispensable."

—DWIGHT D. EISENHOWER[1]

It is hard to imagine how 75 minutes can change the world, but that's what happened on a naval base in Honolulu, Hawaii, on December 7, 1941. More than 2,400 Americans died during the Japanese sneak attack on Pearl Harbor and 1,000 more were injured. Though there had been intelligence briefings that had warned of such an attack, they were ignored because of how implausible and outlandish the possibility seemed. Hawaii is nearly 4,000 miles away from Japan, and no one expected the enemy to be that bold or cunning.

"Missed clues, intelligence errors, and overconfidence."[2] These words most accurately describe what led to the devastating attack on Pearl Harbor. One Rear Admiral and a Lieutenant General responsible for defending Hawaii were charged and found guilty of dereliction of duty in 1942. Regardless of who was to blame, this intelligence failure was devastating.

Ultimately, God took what the enemy meant for evil and turned it around. Japan had hoped that this attack would shock us into dizzied compliance, but instead it strengthened American resolve and thrust us into a long overdue declaration of war.

Stories like these can be very sobering, but they can also make us vulnerable if we focus more on our nation's ability to rally after being attacked than the preparation for war itself. There is no question that "The Greatest Generation" earned their title during these trying times, but their ability to respond to such a devastating attack is the exception and not the rule. Many use these heroic tales in history as some kind of twisted narcotic, allowing them to sleep on, hoping that when the worst comes, they'll be able to bounce back. Often, this is fear masquerading as faith. Though faith can win the war, blind optimism (which often impersonates faith) is a poor substitute that, in the end, will leave us unaware and unprepared.

I believe that no matter what comes, we will overcome by the grace of God. However, placing our heads in the sand and ignoring disturbing intelligence while hoping for the best is no real strategy for a successful Christian life.

True faith can hear and digest the most devastating news and remain unmoved in its resolve to see victory. Many in the church today avoid the prophetic word of God because it awakens them to dangers of which they would rather stay ignorant.

Christians have a dangerous habit of striving to avoid bad news in some misguided attempt to preserve the illusion of faith. Again, faith is never fearful of bad news. Battle-ready faith can take any information or intelligence and use it to strengthen its position.

I have known people who avoided going to the doctor because they were fearful of getting a bad report. Then, they act as though this dereliction of duty somehow displays a deep trust in God. Though we should always be led by the Holy Spirit and good common sense in our dealings with the medical community, faith doesn't fear a bad report. On the contrary, faith can use any negative news it receives to redirect its focus and strategically bombard the enemy. The answer to any bad report could be, "Now we know what we're fighting and how to pray."

Hudson Maxim, an inventor and chemist in the early 20th century, was a genius admired by the likes of Thomas Edison.

Known for inventing a variety of explosives and smokeless gunpowder, he kept his eyes on a simmering conflict that would later be known as "The Great War." As WWI was spreading across the globe, Hudson wrote a very unpopular book titled *Defenseless America*. His hopes were that:

> Possibly this book may lessen a little the effect of the pernicious propagandism of the pacifists....
>
> Pacifism has ringed the nose of the American people and is leading them, blind and unknowing, to the slaughter. War is inevitable... The American people could not now be roused sufficiently to avert the impending calamity even by a call that would rift the sky and shake down the stars from Heaven! Fate has decreed that our pride shall be humbled, and that we shall be bowed to the dirt. We must first put on sackcloth, ashed in the embers of our burning homes. Perhaps when we build anew on the fire-blacked desolation, our mood may be receptive of the knowledge that we must shield our homes with blood and brawn and iron.[3]

Pacifism is, by definition, an opposition to war or violence. War is not an idea that helps us sleep at night. It is easy for us to create blinders to keep from having to consider such an idea. This crippling concept was abounding in the American mindset leading into World War I, and it is just as prominent in the pop-church psychology of our day. Spiritual pacifism has ringed the nose of the modern church.

Don't Shoot the Messenger

Hudson Maxim feared that his warning would fall on deaf ears. Too many undesirables had come before him and used the fear of war to line their own pockets and advance their own agendas. Many in the church today are war-weary if for no other reason than that they have been besieged by masterful marketing techniques masquerading as "evangelism."

Have we become numb to any real call to arms because of the preponderance of warlike language in the contemporary church? Faux warfare has become a fun topic of conversation. With the lucrative promotion of t-shirts, jewelry, books, sermon series, and worship songs on the subject of spiritual warfare, the church has fallen prey to an improper association of real spiritual battle with entertaining sermon illustrations.

Warfare has become fanfare, and in the midst of it all, anyone with a combat message that doesn't match our previous rose-tinted perception is booed off the stage. We're now in this weird RPG (role-playing game) that inspires times of comfort more than it encourages times of preparation for conflict. We must welcome those who awaken us to the real dangers we face and who bring us news we may not think we want to hear.

Like our nation in times past, the church has been hurt by shysters and pious politicians, but Hudson Maxim's words more than 100 years ago still ring true today:

> It is every man's duty, not only to himself, but also to those dear to him, to know the truth about anything which may menace his and their welfare, in order

that he and they may become awakened to the danger and prepare for it accordingly. Those who deceive us by warning us of danger when there is no danger may not do us any harm; in fact, they may even do us good by cultivating our alertness and awareness. The hare may jump at a thousand false alarms to every one of actual danger; but it is the false alarms that have given him the alertness to save himself when real danger comes. On the other hand, those who convince us that there is no danger when there is great danger are the worst of enemies; they expose us, naked of defense, to the armed and armored enemy.... Among the great deceivers with whom the human race has to contend is the confidence man, for he plays upon the fears, vanity, and credulity of his victim.... He enlists his victim with him, and they work together to the same end. No man is greatly deceived by another except through his own cooperation.[4]

This fortifies what we discovered in the last chapter about warfare awareness, but it also takes it a bit further. If we tend to avoid the concept of war, we will deliberately miss out on hearing and heeding much needed warfare intelligence.

Are you willing to hear from God? This is a question that goes much deeper and is far more worrisome when asked another way, "Are you willing to allow God to be honest with you?" God will only unlock His end-time armory to the courageous at heart who are daring enough to participate in this kind of candid covenant with the Father.

A Prophetic Intel Briefing

Now, we are ready for divine intelligence. In the time of Hosea the prophet, the nation of Israel was enjoying a time of outward peace and prosperity. Inwardly, though, they were losing the spiritual war with devastating consequences. Hosea's own marriage was an illustration of the nation's prophetic intelligence failure. Here was God's message of warning to them:

> *My people are destroyed for lack of knowledge: because thou hast rejected knowledge, I will also reject thee, that thou shalt be no priest to me: seeing thou hast forgotten the law of thy God, I will also forget thy children* (Hosea 4:6).

The message is clear: destruction comes when we fail to connect with and heed the knowledge of God. In the same way that a massive intelligence failure led to the surprise attack on the Pacific Fleet at Pearl Harbor, a prophetic intelligence failure can lead to devastating attacks on the church. How many needless attacks have each of us endured simply because we failed to pursue or act on divine intelligence?

I host a program called *Encounter Today*. This amazing platform gives me the opportunity to interview and glean from some amazing ministry gifts. In one interview that I did with Lou Engle, this general of the faith said something that set my spirit on fire. As he was sharing his vision for a mighty movement of prayer and fasting in the church, he said that we are a prayer community that asks God for divine intelligence.

Many carelessly take steps of faith and pray that God will bless their oblivious endeavors, postmortem. Much of our faith is wasted cleaning up messes created by our own ignorance. Thankfully, God's grace is more than sufficient. In fact, I encourage you to take a moment right now and thank Him for His long-suffering toward us.

There are certainly times when we must, as Dr. Lilian B. Yeoman puts it, "step out over the aching void with nothing underneath our feet but the Word of God."[5] However, in these moments, we're not walking on the water. We are walking on His Word. His Word is a means for us to interact with His intellect. This opportunity collects dust on our shelves and remains unwooed and unloved by much of the church. When was the last time you sought God for divine intelligence?

You Don't Need the News

Today, everything has become politicized. The scientific community, social media, our educational systems, and the news have all been weaponized in order to sell us something. Team sports is a lucrative business, and the media has spent considerable effort splitting us into teams and pitting us one against the other.

It has become nearly impossible to get a straight answer about what's really going on around us. Nature despises a vacuum, and this void of truth has been filled by every conspiracy hypothesis imaginable. Since the conspiracy theorists are often more genuine than the news media themselves, many good-hearted Christians have gravitated toward them like moths to a flame.

Like many of you, I used to run to my favorite or most trusted news sources to try and cypher the truth for myself before going to the Word. My excuse for this may sound familiar:

"Well, I need to watch _____ or read _____ so that I can stay up to date on what's happening, and so that I can pray more effectively."

I didn't realize that this mentality exposes our dependence on unreliable sources instead of the Holy Spirit. I was a "news junkie," and the pursuit of my next fix was often keeping me away from the One for whom my soul longed:

I will rise now, and go about the city in the streets, and in the broad ways I will seek him whom my soul loveth: I sought him, but I found him not. The watchmen that go about the city found me: to whom I said, Saw ye him whom my soul loveth? It was but a little that I passed from them, but I found him whom my soul loveth: I held him, and would not let him go (Song of Solomon 3:2-4).

Upon discovering this, I went on a fast that changed my life forever. I fasted all news for more than one entire year. Allow me to clarify that I am not saying that you should never watch the news. I am just sharing what I uncovered and how it can transform your prayer life. The spirit of antichrist is a political spirit, and it will blind the minds of everyone who caters to it. It places us in factions and pits us against each other, ruining our witness with stances that have no chapter or verse attached to them.

The Bible says that *"wine is a mocker"* (Prov. 20:1). This means that alcohol mocks those who think they can control it. As I was praying during this fast, I heard the Lord say, "If wine is a mocker, then politics is a satirist that will turn every believer into a caricature of themselves."

Are we supposed to be involved in politics? Yes, but at the direction of the Holy Spirit. Until we hear from Him, all our political debates will mean nothing when compared to the eternal good that could have come from spending that time and effort being salt and light, teaching men and women to hear the voice of God for themselves. Here's my recommendation: unfollow the partisan hacks on social media and stop watching the fake or the real news if it's keeping you away from the word that God has for you.

If we find Him for whom our soul longs, we'll find the answer to every national woe. We can no longer allow the world to politicize the church when it's the church that's supposed to gospelize the world. Again, I'm not saying we shouldn't be informed and involved, but I am saying we should reevaluate our sources.

Elijah didn't know what was happening in the inner chambers of the enemy king because he was watching the evening news. He wasn't in the spin room; he was in the prayer room.

> *Then the king of Syria warred against Israel, and took counsel with his servants, saying, In such and such a place shall be my camp. And the man of God sent unto the king of Israel, saying, Beware that thou pass not such a place; for thither the Syrians*

*are come down. And the king of Israel sent to the
place which the man of God told him and warned
him of, and saved himself there, not once nor twice.*

*Therefore the heart of the king of Syria was sore
troubled for this thing; and he called his servants,
and said unto them, Will ye not shew me which of
us is for the king of Israel? And one of his servants
said, None, my lord, O king: but Elisha, the prophet
that is in Israel, telleth the king of Israel the words
that thou speakest in thy bedchamber. And he said,
Go and spy where he is* (2 Kings 6:8-13).

Did you notice that this war with the Syrians was a war of
intelligence? The war that you are in right now is such a war.
From Genesis to Revelation, we see an epic battle between light
and darkness. The allusions in scripture to *light* or the condem-
nations we find of *darkness* have less to do with electromagnetic
radiation than they do with the possession of knowledge. It will
help you immensely if, whenever you read the word *light* in the
Bible, you immediately connect it to "revelation knowledge."
Conversely, when you read the word *darkness*, add to it *ignorance*.

The very first spiritual battle—in the Garden of Eden—was
fought over the knowledge of good and evil (see Gen. 3). The
enemy wants to blind you to God's intelligence. To be blinded,
in this sense, is to be made ignorant of divine intelligence; to be
a partaker of the light is to receive revelation knowledge.

*But if our gospel be hid, it is hid to them that are
lost: in whom the god of this world hath blinded the*

*minds of them which believe not, lest the light of the
glorious gospel of Christ, who is the image of God,
should shine unto them* (2 Corinthians 4:3-4).

Military intelligence can shift the battle. With the right
knowledge, a small resistance can overcome an overwhelming
foe. With the right word, defeated troops can snatch victory
from the jaws of defeat.

God stands ready to impart divine intelligence to every war-
weary saint reading this book today. Just one word from Him
can cool the fevered brow of an infant child. Just one word
from Him can calm the seas of anxiety raging in your mind.
Just one word from Him can stupefy the fear that has paralyzed
you. This is the power resident in the real prophetic word. The
prophet Isaiah understood this concept:

> *The Lord God hath given me the tongue of the
> learned, that I should know how to speak a word in
> season to him that is weary: he wakeneth morning
> by morning, he wakeneth mine ear to hear as the
> learned* (Isaiah 50:4).

A prophetic word is simply a "right now" word; it is a living
word. A prophetic word is when the sword of the Lord comes
alive and pierces the moment. When this happens, death has to
loose its hold, and darkness has to flee. Divine intelligence—
also called *revelation*—is our greatest weapon against the enemy
in spiritual warfare.

Have you ever had a moment when the words seemed to
jump off the pages of your Bible? Have you ever heard a sermon

or a song that seemed to be aimed straight at your heart? What's happening in these moments? God is providing relevant, timely, tactical support for the battle in which you are engaged.

In the next chapter, we are going to discover how God's Word can open prayer portals through which His military provisions can be transferred to His church. But first, I need you to recognize that things are already beginning to change in your life while you are reading these words. God has already begun to strengthen your faith, and He is imparting divine intelligence to you right now.

As I'm writing, I can hear the word of God for you, saying: "Your warfare has *shifted!* You are about to go from *rout* to *rally*. The tables have turned, and what the enemy has been to you, you are about to become to him. Your fighting spirit is being restored and you are about to go from bunker building to bunker busting!"

I challenge you to take a moment and rejoice over that word from the Lord. What does it mean?

> *Rout:* the panicked and disorderly retreat of troops on the verge of defeat. It creates a herd mentality that drives groups to retreat to a place of imagined safety.
>
> *Rally:* the opposite of rout. A force on the brink of defeat is instilled with a fighting spirit.

Your warfare has shifted, and your fighting spirit is being revived right now. Throughout history, in moments of seeming defeat, it is sometimes surprising what can be used as a rallying cry. Fredrick the Great in 1757 rallied his troops by saying, "Scoundrels, do you want to live forever?"[6]

Brigadier General Norman Cota on Omaha Beach said, "Gentlemen, we are being killed on the beaches. Let us go inland and be killed."[7]

These words turned the tide and fortified the spines of those facing imminent death. From "Banzai" to "Geronimo" or from the Rebel Yell to "Remember the Alamo," a rallying cry often comes from a victorious declaration of faith.

God is releasing a word in season to all those who are prepared to hear it. It may not seem possible, and all the evidence may be to the contrary, but if we can hear it, the battle can turn. Here is the greatest rallying cry from the lips of the greatest Victor: *"It is finished"* (John 19:30)!

Notes

1. David Giltner, "Plans Are Useless, but Planning Is Indispensable, TurningScience, March 28, 2021, https://turningscience.com/planning-is-indispensable.

2. Carl Gnam and Wayne Kurth, "Pearl Harbor Attack Cover-Up," Warfare History Network, January 4, 2020, https://warfarehistorynetwork.com/2020/01/04/pearl-harbor-attack-cover-up.

3. Hudson Maxim, *Defenseless America* (New York: Hearst, 1916), vii-viii.

4. Ibid., xiv.

5. Kenneth E. Hagin, "What It Means to Believe with the Heart (Part II)," HopeFaithPrayer, September

20, 2021, https://www.hopefaithprayer.com/faith/
kenneth-hagin-faith-lesson-no-9-what-it-means-to
-believe-with-the-heart-part-ii.

6. Staff, "Book Review: *Frederick the Great* (by
Giles McDonough)," HistoryNet, August 10,
2016, https://www.historynet.com/book-review
-frederick-the-great-by-giles-mcdonough-mh.htm.

7. "Remembering BG Norman 'Dutch' Cota, One of
the D-Day Heroes," SOFREP, June 7, 2021, https://
sofrep.com/specialoperations/remembering-bg
-norman-dutch-cota-one-of-the-d-day-heroes.

CHAPTER FOUR

PRAYER PORTALS

Jesus answered, My kingdom is not of this world.
—JOHN 18:36

"But do you really mean, sir," said Peter, "that there could be other worlds—all over the place, just round the corner—like that?" "Nothing is more probable," said the Professor, taking off his spectacles and beginning to polish them, while he muttered to himself, "I wonder what they do teach them at these schools."
—C.S. LEWIS,
The Lion, the Witch and the Wardrobe,[1]

Rations and Communications

Crucial to every army's survival—from Attila the Hun to modern special forces—are reliable intelligence and a steady supply of rations. Without the latter, an army can starve, even though they have superior training and equipment. In our spiritual battle, God supernaturally supplies both intelligence and sustenance through His Word.

His Word provides both manna and meaning. It nurtures equally the body and the soul (see Matt. 4:4). Prayer is the means by which we open a portal or supply line to Heaven's resources.

Secular scientists are now asking if we could be living side by side with a parallel universe. If you are a Bible believer, you know that there is an entire unseen world all around us. What if there are portals, doorways, or bridges that could connect us with that other world? This may seem like science fiction, but much of what is common science today was at one time considered science fiction.

From space travel to robotic arms, cell phones, and the internet, we're surrounded by what would have been considered the impossible just a few years ago.

Are there parallel universes? Is it possible to open a doorway that could give us access to the resources available there? I'm borrowing these secular terms in the hopes that it will help you to see this truth in a new light. We're not getting into some kind of new age, metaphysical doublespeak here. We're just hijacking the secular conversation and using their terms to communicate Bible truth.

The reality of another world living next to ours is one readily accepted by many secular authorities. Eric Weinstein, a mathematician and commentator, justifies his belief in a multiverse by referencing our common mythology. Throughout history, our literature is filled with allusions to doorways to another world. Whether it's the rabbit hole in *Alice in Wonderland*, the wardrobe in *The Chronicles of Narnia*, or the red pill in the *Matrix*, we find this powerful narrative repeated again and again. Could this universal fascination with finding a portal to another world be rooted in reality?

Today, the concept of a parallel universe and the discovery of actual portals or access points is moving from fringe science to regular studies in many laboratories all over the world. Not long ago, the reputable Oak Ridge National Laboratory in Tennessee conducted major experiments in an attempt to open a doorway to another universe.

What many in the scientific community don't realize is that we already have a portal—a stargate—to another world: prayer! This revelation is essential for us to remain armed for victory in our lives.

Jacob's Ladder

And Jacob went out from Beersheba, and went toward Haran. And he lighted upon a certain place, and tarried there all night, because the sun was set; and he took of the stones of that place, and put them for his pillows, and lay down in that place to sleep. And he dreamed, and behold a ladder set up on the earth, and the top of it reached to heaven: and behold the angels of God ascending and descending on it. And, behold, the Lord stood above it, and said, I am the Lord God of Abraham thy father, and the God of Isaac: the land whereon thou liest, to thee will I give it, and to thy seed; and thy seed shall be as the dust of the earth, and thou shalt spread abroad to the west, and to the east, and to the north, and to the south: and in thee and in thy seed shall all the families of the earth be blessed. And, behold, I am with thee, and will keep thee in all places whither thou goest, and will bring thee again into this land; for I will not leave thee, until I have done that which I have spoken to thee of. And Jacob awaked out of his sleep, and he said, Surely the Lord is in this place; and I knew it not. And he was afraid, and said, How dreadful is this place! this is none other but the house of God, and this is the gate of heaven (Genesis 28:10-17).

Jacob found a bridge to another world, and his life was changed as a result. When we learn how to open these portals and build these bridges, God's miraculous supply becomes easily accessible.

When my church discovered this truth, effortless miracles began to take place in our prayer meetings. What I mean by *effortless* is that we didn't have to try to make anything happen. When God shows up, the enemy flees. When God shows up, whatever is wrong is made right. An open portal is a weapon. If you want to be armed for victory, you need to find or create a gateway to Heaven like Jacob did.

An Open Heaven Is a Powerful Weapon

Supernatural deliverance and healing started to break out in these prayer services. In one instance, a gentleman had been so tormented by demon spirits that he had attempted suicide. His first attempt had failed, and his wife was rushing him to the hospital. On the way, he tried to throw himself out of the car.

The road to the hospital went right past our church. It happened that we were holding a prayer meeting that night. When the wife saw that the church lights were on, she pulled into the parking lot. In desperation, she kicked him out of the car and drove off. She didn't know what else to do!

He came in to make a call but found out that Jesus was already on the main line! The worship and the prayer in the room were so sincere and faith-filled that a portal had been opened. A bridge had been built that could deliver this man's miracle straight to him. The moment he walked in, the presence of God hit him. He was instantly delivered and set free. As a result, he rededicated his life to the Lord.

This was only possible because real prayer was being offered in that place. Real prayer opens a portal and builds a bridge. Prayer is more than a casual conversation between two friends. It's a system, instituted by God, to bridge the gap between Heaven and earth. Prayer constructs a bridge between two worlds. If we continue to use secular terminology, we would say that prayer, done properly, causes a trans-dimensional rift that creates a tear in the fabric of space-time. What a bridge!

Each one of us is tasked with growing in our relationship with God and our understanding of His Word in order to build this bridge. How we build it will determine what we receive from Heaven. There are different kinds of bridges: log bridges, beam bridges, trusses, arches, viaducts, cables, suspensions. Each one is constructed with a purpose. That purpose is based on what we plan to transport over it. Militaries throughout history have been required to learn how to build these kinds of bridges if they wish to survive. When planning a bridge, the architect must first ask, "What do I need to transport over this bridge?"

As a kid, I played in a park near my home. A small creek with a single-log bridge ran through the park. It wasn't easy to get across—only one person could go at a time. We loved trying to knock each other off balance as we tried to cross the log. Even though we usually managed to get across, I wouldn't recommend attempting to carry a TV or a mattress over that log. It wasn't made for that.

When we begin to think about our prayer lives, we have to ask ourselves: what do we plan to receive from Heaven? What kind of bridge have we built with our current prayer life? Is it big enough to carry national revival, or can we barely get our own needs met with it? Is it sturdy enough to transport our healing from Heaven to earth? Is it solid enough to convey Heaven's weapons for the war we're facing?

The Bible says that before a man goes to war, he should count the cost. The bridge we construct depends on the size, weight, and frequency of delivery. Is your prayer life ready to convey Heaven's armored tank division? It will be before you finish this book!

This thing called "prayer" is much bigger than we realize. In order to open this prayer portal and strengthen this bridge, we must first understand the true nature of prayer. In my book *Encounter: Are You Ready to Experience More of God's Power and Presence*, I share some of these basics. I want to reiterate a few of those key points and then share something truly fresh and revolutionary with you.

The Essence of True Prayer

In order to understand prayer—the true nature of prayer— it would help if we would just forget everything we think we know about the subject. Much of what we call prayer in today's Americanized, bumper-sticker, Christian philosophy of prayer can be broken up into several distinct categories:

The Negotiator's Prayer: The Negotiator attempts to bribe God by offering Him a great deal: "God, if You'll just get me out of this, I promise to go to church this Sunday!"

The Blackmailer's Prayer: The Blackmailer isn't as polite as the Negotiator. He's done playing nice with God, and now he's determined to make God an offer He can't refuse: "God, if You don't answer this prayer, I'll never go to church again!"

The Pious Prayer: The Pious Prayer is generally offered exclusively for the sake of an audience. Whether it's with a church group, over Thanksgiving dinner, or solely for your conscience's sake, the purpose of this prayer is to make others think you are spiritual or holy. You can tell if you're guilty of praying this type of prayer if you're unable to recall the prayer you prayed two minutes after you say *amen*.

The Pity Prayer: The Pity Prayer is probably the most popular of all the nonstarters. "Lord, I'm so desperate; if You don't do something, I'm not going to make it!" This prayer feels the need to show God pictures of malnourished children, the crumbling foundations of our homes, or the buckets of tears we've shed. After all, if we can "sell" God on how desperate our need is, He will have to respond, right?[2]

Wrong, wrong, wrong! God is not looking to make a deal, associate with religious icons, or listen to a sales pitch. God is looking for worshipers. God is looking for people who will make His presence their priority and who will consider time with Him more precious than silver or gold.

When we take the time to worship Him first, we will sense the presence of God right there where we are. At times, God's presence will come to us like a rushing wind or a mighty fire, and at other times, it will come as a still small voice or an inner witness. Either way, we will know that God is near.

Once we have the assurance and peace that comes from knowing that God is near, it's time to speak the Word. We must be careful not to begin to speak our own words. The Holy Spirit is like a dove, and He is very particular about where He rests. Our Creator is looking for someone to agree with:

> *Can two walk together, except they be agreed?*
> (Amos 3:3)

Remember when Jesus was walking with His disciples along the coast of Caesarea Philippi (Matt. 16:15) and He asked them,

"Who do you say that I am?" What was the purpose of this question? Did Jesus have amnesia? Did He forget who He was? Of course not! He was looking for someone to agree with Him, because agreement is the way He gains access into our lives.

According to Genesis 1 and Psalm 8, God placed us in authority in the earth. Therefore, if God desires to do anything significant in the earth, He must get us to agree with Him. This is the purpose of prayer! Our heavenly Father needs to find someone to say, *"Thy will be done in earth, as it is in heaven"* (Matt. 6:10).

Agreement with God is the essence of true prayer. All prayer must begin with the Word of God; the desired end of each prayer must be the fulfillment of the will of God. Unless we grasp this simple principle, we will not find much success in prayer. Prayer is all about agreeing with God and His Word.

We must learn to speak God's words and not our own. As we prepare for prayer, the Bible verses we need don't always suddenly come to us out of the blue. We can prepare for success in prayer by writing down the verses that articulate the will of God for our lives. Once the presence of God shows up, we can begin to speak those verses aloud and praise God for His Word.

Learning His Ways

Getting into the presence of God is easy. God desires to be with us so much more than we desire to be with Him. He has made all the preparations and stands ready to greet us. Abiding in the presence of God can be effortless—if we first learn His ways. Here is what God says:

"I don't think the way you think. The way you work isn't the way I work." God's Decree. "For as the sky soars high above earth, so the way I work surpasses the way you work, and the way I think is beyond the way you think. Just as rain and snow descend from the skies and don't go back until they've watered the earth, doing their work of making things grow and blossom, producing seed for farmers and food for the hungry, so will the words that come out of my mouth not come back empty-handed. They'll do the work I sent them to do, they'll complete the assignment I gave them" (Isaiah 55:8-11 MSG).

Learning His ways, seeking His face, and experiencing His glory is what it's all about. However, many never get over the first hurdle of learning His ways, and they become like *"broken cisterns, that can hold no water"* (Jer. 2:13).

Without an understanding of the ways of God, we are nothing more than fractured vessels that cannot contain the glory of God. It's said that if you give a man a fish you can feed him for a day, but if you teach a man to fish you can feed him for a lifetime. Instead of looking for a quick fix, we must learn to sustain spiritual things. Accidental victory is no guarantee of future success.

In times of distress, loss, or grief, we will invariably hear pious parrots squawking on about how His ways are not our ways, and His thoughts are not our thoughts. To these folks, divine transcendence is something to be admired, but this gap between humanity and deity is nothing to be praised. The breach between God's ways and our ways is a problem, not a providence. This fissure is the reason for creation's chaos, yet many quote it as though it should provide some sort of comfort for the confused. We hear things like, "In this time of loss, it's difficult to understand, but His ways are not our ways."

This direct disregard of doctrine would almost be tolerable if it weren't so preposterous. In this verse, God, through Isaiah, clearly explains that there is a cure for this malady of separation: the Word! It is true that God's thoughts are heavenly while ours are often grounded, but, just as rain and snow descend from the skies and don't go back until they've watered the earth, so God will send His Word. Effective prayer that can build a bridge must be based on God's Word.

What, then, is a word? A word is a thought communicated. God, in His grace, bridges the gap between His thoughts and our thoughts with His Word. Now, we can make His ways our ways through the revelation of the Word of God. Isn't that what the gospel is all about? God sent His Son—the Word made flesh—to bridge the gap. How do we stay on track when we're seeking God in prayer? The Word. How do we align our thoughts with His? The Word. The Word must saturate our prayer life. When the Word is not only the basis of our prayers, but the answer to them as well, we're on our way to victory.

A Holy Invitation

If we want to increase the scope of what our prayers can carry from Heaven to Earth, we must learn to revere the truly awesome invitation we've been given. Prayer is communication with God.

When we see this for what it is, we will begin to appreciate that prayer is more than telling God what we need. In fact, if prayer is communication with God, then prayer began long before man ever uttered a word.

> *And God said, Let us make man in our image, after our likeness: and let them have dominion over the fish of the sea, and over the fowl of the air, and over the cattle, and over all the earth, and over every creeping thing that creepeth upon the earth* (Genesis 1:26).

In the oneness of the Trinity, God is communicating with Himself when He says let "Us" make man in Our image. Here we see a communication or communion within the Trinity itself. Prayer is taking place between the Father, the Son, and the Holy Spirit. Prayer originates in the Trinity, and through Jesus and faith in His name, we are invited into that holy communion. Prayer is our invitation into the inner workings of the Trinity.

> *But ye, beloved, building up yourselves on your most holy faith, praying in the Holy Ghost* (Jude 20).

The Holy Spirit is communing with the Father, and when we pray as instructed, we tune in to the divine communications between them. This is a mighty weapon that we have taken for granted.

The reason people tend to be fascinated with the science fiction concepts of portals or stargates is because they illustrate truths that, deep within ourselves, we know exist. All of this can be found in the Word and in prayer. In order for God's army to be armed for victory, we must learn to tap into this sacred truth. Heaven's resources are all around us.

> *From that time Jesus began to preach, and to say, Repent: for the kingdom of heaven is at hand* (Matthew 4:17).

The Kingdom of Heaven is within your reach right now. Build a bridge through faith-filled prayer and worship that your victory can cross over.

Notes

1. C. S. Lewis, *The Lion, the Witch, and the Wardrobe* (Scholastic, 1994).

2. Alan Didio, *Encounter: Are You Ready to Experience More of God's Power and Presence* (2018).

CHAPTER FIVE

THE EVOLUTION OF WARFARE

How are the mighty fallen, and the weapons of war perished!

—2 SAMUEL 1:27

"The sword of the Spirit in another person's hand will not defend you."

—WILLIAM GURNALL[1]

Prayer is often ignored in the modern church while spiritual warfare is prostituted and commercialized to such an extent that both would be unrecognizable to the apostle Paul. Rarely do the two ever come together in a way that can benefit the average Christian or our society. Let's take a look at the weapon of prayer and how it has evolved over the last century. These principles will radically transform our prayer lives:

> *And it came to pass, that, as he was praying in a certain place, when he ceased, one of his disciples said unto him, Lord, teach us to pray, as John also taught his disciples. And he said unto them, When ye pray, say, Our Father which art in heaven, Hallowed be thy name. Thy kingdom come. Thy will be done, as in heaven, so in earth* (Luke 11:1-2).

Going Beyond the Formula

Prayer begins as a model with a specific recipe. The very idea of a prayer formula makes many Charismatics cringe. This is understandable, especially for someone who was previously bound by religious tradition. Some equate dead religion with rote memorization and want nothing to do with it. "Let the Spirit flow!" They want it all to flow spontaneously, but real power-filled extemporaneous prayer is birthed out of this kind of recipe. A good formula can serve as a great foundation.

In the Old Testament, there were different sacrifices that had to be offered in specific ways. Once that formula was honored, God would move on someone's heart to say, "Be healed" or "Rain cease." In the New Testament, before Jesus or His disciples declaratively spoke deliverance or healing, the foundation was invoked first, *"Our Father which art in heaven"* (see Matt 6:5-15).

There are people who want to oversimplify prayer; there are people who want to overcomplicate it. However, prayer is both simple and complicated. Those who proclaim its simplicity generally lack discipline, and those who declare its complexity generally lack grace. There is a secret place somewhere in the middle. It begins by learning everything we can about prayer and building a scriptural foundation, and it ends with simply allowing the Holy Spirit to pray through us.

Prayer for the sick can be as simple as saying, "Arise, take up your bed and walk," but no one should be deceived into believing that it started there. No, it starts with preparation, study, and discipline. Not just on our part, but on the part of those who went before us. For every public demonstration of power-filled prayer we see, there are hours of private practice in the presence of God that we do not see. Our problem is that we long for the victories we see in others without being willing to be faithful to the formulas that produced them.

Arm Miraculously Healed

In 1998, I was taking a tour of a Bible college. My small group of eight people walked into the college's prayer center. We could feel the presence of God when we stepped into the room. Here, people called in from all over the world to receive prayer. Twenty-four hours a day, this team of prayer warriors prayed for the needs of thousands around the world, seven days a week. There was an elderly gentleman who was given the task of showing us around. Later, he would become my mentor in prayer.

Over time, I learned that this man was so consumed with a love for God and a divine compassion that he never allowed a need to go without prayer. If he ever saw a need or sensed that someone required prayer, he would not hesitate to reach out to them and speak the Word of God over them.

It just so happened that one of the gentlemen in my group had such a need. When he was just a toddler, he had been hit by a Mack truck. Miraculously, he survived—but his arm was locked in what seemed like a ninety-degree angle. Even after multiple surgeries, he could not stretch his arm out straight.

This elderly statesman in the faith noticed the infirmity and inquired about it. After hearing the story, he began to speak to the young man's arm. He prayed in a way I had never heard before. Speaking to the ligaments and calling the muscles out by their medical names, he talked so fast I could hardly understand him. All I could clearly comprehend at the end of the prayer was when he looked at the boy and told him to "stretch it out." Guess what happened? He stretched it out! After more than 15 years, this young man received his healing and went praising God around the building!

Everyone was watching the boy, but my eyes stayed on this man of faith. While those in the room who witnessed the miracle were celebrating, my soon-to-be mentor quietly walked back to his desk, picked up the phone, and started praying for someone else like nothing had happened! To us, it was the greatest miracle we had ever seen, but to him it was Thursday. I determined in that moment that I wanted to learn how to pray like that.

I began to volunteer with him and asked if I could just follow him around and listen to him pray. I learned that to him, answered prayer was normal. I would take notes and write down how he prayed and then apply it when I would pray for others.

When I applied his method, I saw his results. People would be miraculously healed.

I have heard it said—and it's true—that the greatest discoveries of the 20th century were not in science or technology, but in prayer. We have seen prayer evolve over the past 100 years back to what I believe God intended it to be. We're not there yet, but we're getting there. Before the outpouring of the Holy Spirit in the early 20th century, prayer had one primary function—repentance. This understanding began to evolve throughout the first quarter of that century.

During the depression, a minister in Minnesota named Glen Clark developed schools of prayer called "Camp Farthest Out." More than seventy people gathered for an extended period to learn how to pray. Professor Clark modeled the camp after football camps. People were encouraged to try new ways of praying. He had people practice praying for one another.

This, you must understand, was a drastic divergence from the grandiose nature of prayer to which most were accustomed. Prayer was something either done in secret or declared eloquently by trained clergy. Before this, the only type of prayer most knew anything about was the prayer of repentance—yet now, they were learning how to petition Heaven for the most practical things in the most practical ways.

The Happy Hunters

Glen Clark is just one example of how the Spirit of God was moving the church to evolve in its understanding of prayer. In a few short years, we evolved from repentance to powerful petitions.

As God continued to open His arsenal, the prayer of petition became the norm and not the exception. It seems to take a least a quarter of a century for the church to grasp a new prayer concept. After fifty years, we tend to take things to extremes or take them for granted. A hundred years later, we could use another revival of the prayer of repentance as a chief weapon in our arsenal.

As the prayer of petition became more common and acceptable, God brought forward a couple named Charles and Frances Hunter. They would later be called "The Happy Hunters." A new kind of prayer was burning in their hearts—the commanding prayer.

There are times when we speak *to* God, and there are other times when we speak *for* God. This is "commanding prayer."

> *When you enter a town and are welcomed, eat what is offered to you. Heal the sick who are there and tell them, "The kingdom of God has come near to you." ...The seventy-two returned with joy and said, "Lord, even the demons submit to us in your name"* (Luke 10:8-9,17 NIV).

It was obvious to the Hunters that whenever the disciples encountered sickness or demonic oppression, they confronted it with a command. Remnants of this commanding authority remain today, even in the most religious circles. The Catholic Church still has thousands of exorcists who are taught to command demons to leave. If we're still casting out demons in the modern church, why are we "asking" for sickness to leave with the prayer of petition?

The Hunters understood that every follower of Jesus had the authority and duty to command sickness to leave just like they would command demons to leave. They taught that command healing was the birthright of every believer, and not just those especially gifted like many of the great tent evangelists in history. This was for everyone.

In 1981, the Hunters published their now classic work, *How to Heal the Sick*. The Hunters put together crusades they called "Healing Explosions," where they trained hundreds of people to minister these commanding prayers throughout an audience of thousands! Their plan was simple—"teach, model, and do."

Outstanding Christian historian and dear friend, Dr. William DeArteaga, has provided their history in a tremendous article titled, "The Happy Hunter's Revolution in Healing Prayer." Here is a portion of that article:

> The Hunters continued to search out any new scraps of information that would be of help in the healing ministry. They had a panel of medical doctors and chiropractors who advised them and keep them posted on new medical discoveries. For instance, in recent years medical investigators have discovered that human cells give out faint electrical pulses, but that cancer cells give out significantly different and disharmonious frequencies. The Hunters encouraged the following prayer over cancer victims:
>
> Devil, I bind you right now by the Spirit of God in Jesus' name. You foul spirit of cancer, I command you to come out right now in the name of Jesus. ...

We speak a new immune system into you and we also speak a new blood system so that the cancer cannot spread any further. We command all of the electrical and chemical frequencies in every cell in your body to be in harmony and in balance and digest the bad cells in Jesus' name.[2]

In just eighty years, the weapon of prayer had evolved from repentance to petition, and then to an understanding of commanding authority in prayer.

The Hunters' spiritual revelations of commanding prayer mirrored changes that were taking place in the natural world. When they met and began their ministry, the '70s were a time of change, with innovations in technology and media, as well as changes in the world military scene post-Vietnam. The evolving revelation the Hunters introduced concerning commanding prayer can be seen as a spiritual representation of the global changes taking place in the world in that era.

The Evolution of Warfare

From the bow and arrow to the machine gun and the unmanned aerial vehicle, the weapons of our warfare are constantly evolving. The tactics of our warfare are also evolving. These innovations in combat change the world. With every revolutionary shift in warfare methodology or machinery, the lines on the world map are redrawn to suit the victors.

Throughout history, horses were essential in warfare until they began to be phased out in World War I. With the use of trenches, barbed wire, the first automatic machine gun, and the tank, the majestic war horse was rendered almost useless on the front lines. Weapons and methods are constantly evolving together to bring about drastic and sweeping changes.

I'm going to share a secret with you that few ever understand about spiritual warfare: *our natural weapons evolve right along with our spiritual ones.* Spiritual warfare is a progressive revelation. I will prove this to you from the Word of God, but first I need you to understand one key principle and never forget it:

That which we see in the natural world is a reflection of that which already exists in the spiritual world.

Mankind is positioned between two realms—the seen and the unseen. These two dimensions are in no way equal in scope. The unseen is far more influential and enduring than the seen. In Hebrews 11:3, Paul says that *"things which are seen are not made of things which do appear."* By this we understand that everything that we can see was made by the unseen. It all started in the spirit first. This unseen and spiritual realm encircles and permeates every part of the seen and natural world.

> *While we look not at the things which are seen,*
> *but at the things which are not seen: for the things*
> *which are seen are temporal; but the things which*
> *are not seen are eternal* (2 Corinthians 4:18).

Spiritual things influence natural things. We all know what it looks like in someone's life when they truly give their hearts to Jesus. Their physical appearance, their work habits, and their relationships change. When I gave my life to Jesus, some of the most surprising changes were my grades in school. I didn't suddenly become a straight-A student, but my scores improved because something had changed in my spiritual life. The spiritual affected the natural. The developments people saw on the outside of my life had their roots in an unseen spiritual development on the inside.

Conversely, what happens when people walk away from God? What happens when someone gives themselves over to an unclean spirit? They live unclean lives in the natural. What happens to a nation in the natural when the church backslides in the spirit? I truly believe that learning to connect natural problems with their spiritual root causes is one of the biggest keys to operating in the prophetic.

When we look at abortion, for example, could it be that there is a root spiritual cause that has produced this American holocaust? I believe that we have aborted a multitude of spiritual infants because of our own hedonistic drive for personal pleasure. How many times have our spirits urged us to go on an outreach or spend time discipling a new believer, but we chose to go to the movies instead? As a church we must fight for the rights of the unborn politically, socially, and legislatively, but if we do not address the root issues, it will all be for nothing. What is the root issue?

In the natural, we see a culture that's addicted to the pleasure of creating life while having an aversion to sustaining it. We want the thrill without the responsibility. Where did this come from? It came from a church that got intoxicated with the excitement of *revival* but didn't want the obligation of *discipleship*. We love the exhilaration of our outreaches and the thrill of our revival services, but we have abandoned the responsibility of raising our spiritual children. If we truly addressed this root, we would eliminate the natural fruit (see Isa. 37:3).

The same could be said about every other personal or national issue. From immigration to low worker participation, all these things are a reflection of something that has been happening in the spirit. Once we realize this, our eyes will be opened to see beyond the seen.

From the invention of the telephone to the advancement of the automobile, these developments have their roots in spiritual innovations. You'll find a striking correlation between these natural inventions and historical revivals within the church. Is this a coincidence, or is every technological advancement the result of some spiritual development that came first? The answer is obvious: spiritual things influence natural things.

The advancement of natural warfare is only made possible by the evolution of revelation regarding spiritual warfare. As God makes new and revelatory understandings of spiritual warfare available to the church, we see shifts in our natural military's conceptions of combat.

In the last century, we saw the development of weapons that have the capacity to destroy the planet or even shift the earth off its axis. Could it be that at the same time, God has been releasing weapons to the church that have the capacity to turn this world upside down? It's thrilling to consider when you look at the evidence of history.

Spiritual warfare must be a progressive revelation because the intensity of the enemy's attacks will increase progressively in the last days.

> *Therefore rejoice, ye heavens, and ye that dwell in them. Woe to the inhabiters of the earth and of the sea! for the devil is come down unto you, having great wrath, because he knoweth that he hath but a short time* (Revelation 12:12).

The Bible even speaks of a time when demon spirits that haven't been seen since the flood will be released on the earth in the last days (see Rev. 9). There's much that could be said here, but what I want you to see is that as we get closer and closer to the return of Jesus, our warfare will intensify. The end-time church may have to deal with demon spirits and an intensity of spiritual attacks that even the apostle Paul never had to deal with. Yet the solution is the same.

Paul's Progressive Revelation

In our study of spiritual warfare, we tend to rally around the apostle Paul's grand opus on the subject. In Ephesians 6, we find a beautifully tailored teaching surrounding the Roman armor of the day. Rivers of ink and mountains of paper have been used to write and expound on Paul's teaching. When Paul says in Ephesians 6:16 to take *"the shield of faith,"* we understand what he means—to a degree. But oh, the revelation that comes when we learn about the intricate details of the Roman shield. I've written about this in my book *The Ephesian Mandate*. There is no limit to the depths of understanding that can be discovered when you begin to peel back the layers of Paul's cultural understanding of war.

Amazingly, this was not the apostle's first foray into teaching on the armor of God. More than a decade earlier, he had begun to mine the depths of this warfare revelation when writing to the Thessalonians:

But let us, who are of the day, be sober, putting on the breastplate of faith and love; and for an helmet, the hope of salvation (1 Thessalonians 5:8).

When we compare this teaching with the one he gave ten years later to the Ephesians, we can see how this revelation grew from just two pieces of armor to more than six—it was a progressive revelation. This is proven even further when you discover that he's quoting from the book of Isaiah!

For he put on righteousness as a breastplate, and an helmet of salvation upon his head; and he put on the garments of vengeance for clothing, and was clad with zeal as a cloak (Isaiah 59:17).

When envisioning the armor of God, Isaiah's readers would have probably thought about the Babylonian armor of the day. A lot had changed in more than 700 years since the prophet wrote these words. And yet, Paul picks them up and applies them to the modern armor of his day.

What's the lesson? God uses contemporary military technology to teach His church how to fight in the spirit. As our access to God's armory grows, there is a concurrent increase in the world's military hardware. Our understanding of faith can now go beyond the Roman shield as we discover hidden parallels in modern security systems from Kevlar to ballistic missile defense.

We never leave these divinely inspired teachings from Paul, nor do we graduate from them with some higher spiritual idea that rivals their inspiration. This would be heresy. They are our foundations and our guiding light as we grow in our understanding of spiritual warfare. However, we must begin to understand that there is a vast armory of divine weapons being made available to us. Every natural military advancement is a calling for us to graduate to a new level of spiritual warfare.

Commanded to Take Command

Isaiah's calling was a difficult one. God essentially told him that he was called to preach a message that no one would listen to:

> *Go and tell this people: "Listen hard, but you aren't going to get it; look hard, but you won't catch on"* (Isaiah 6:9 MSG).

The Word of God can either open people's hearts or it can close them. It can bring them closer or push them farther away. When it's declared in all its prophetic power, they will not be able to stay the same.

It's no wonder Isaiah said, "How long do I have to preach with no one listening?" (see Isa. 6:11). After 40 years of seeming failure, any rational person would conclude that Isaiah's ministry was a failure—but centuries later, when Jesus opened His mouth to preach His first sermon, He quoted Isaiah:

And there was delivered unto him the book of the prophet Esaias. And when he had opened the book, he found the place where it was written, The Spirit of the Lord is upon me, because he hath anointed me to preach the gospel to the poor; he hath sent me to heal the brokenhearted, to preach deliverance to the captives, and recovering of sight to the blind, to set at liberty them that are bruised, to preach the acceptable year of the Lord. And he closed the book, and he gave it again to the minister, and sat down. And the eyes of all them that were in the synagogue were fastened on him (Luke 4:17-20).

What an endorsement! There are times when you may feel like your work for God is getting you nowhere. Be encouraged. Your reward is based on your obedience, not on the outcome or the results.

Isaiah was, as all prophets are, committed to the Word of God. He was committed to doing whatever God told him to do. With that in mind, let's look at Isaiah 45:9: *"Woe unto him that striveth with his maker."*

The sin and folly of resisting God and His commands is just as prevalent today as it was then. The infinite holiness and wisdom of God must be acknowledged for Him to be glorified. He is not to be questioned, second-guessed, or undermined. He is Yahweḥ, Elohim, our Maker.

The immediate reference of the text is those who murmured at the delay of their deliverance from exile and complained about the deliverer whom God chose to send. They thought that God should have delivered them much sooner and that the deliverer should have arisen from among themselves—not as a heathen prince. Many parallels can be drawn from this today.

They criticized God's method. Criticism is a spirit unworthy of the Kingdom of God. Some people always have something negative to say. It's easy to say what's wrong, but it takes a man or woman of God to find what's right.

They criticized, they condemned, and they even worked against God's plan. Bad opinions always lead to bad conduct. Saul of Tarsus is a great example of this.

Before his conversion, he allowed his critical spirit to push him into persecuting Christians. Many people are working against the Lord and aren't even aware that they have set themselves at enmity with the King of Kings.

We must align our thoughts with God's thoughts:

> *And it shall come to pass, if thou shalt hearken diligently unto the voice of the Lord thy God, to observe and to do all his commandments which I command thee this day, that the Lord thy God will set thee on high above all nations of the earth: And all these blessings shall come on thee, and overtake thee, if thou shalt hearken unto the voice of the Lord thy God* (Deuteronomy 28:1-2).
>
> *If ye love me, keep my commandments* (John 14:15).

Isaiah embraced these truths; we would do well to also embrace them:

- God demands compliance even when it's carnally uncomfortable.

- God demands obedience even when it's traditionally untenable.

- God demands submission even when it's practically impossible.

Here are some biblical examples of these three truths. The prophet Ezekiel was commanded to lie on his side for a year covered in animal dung (see Ezek. 4:4). God commanded him to do something carnally uncomfortable. In the Gospel of Mark, we see Jesus order a man with a withered hand to "stretch it out" (see Mark 3:1-6). God commanded him to do what was physically impossible for him so that he could receive what was naturally impossible. In Acts 10, the apostle Peter is commanded to eat unclean animals. God commanded him to do something that was legally and traditionally untenable (see Acts 10:9-16). What's the lesson?

Don't resist God! When approaching a command from God, we must remember that "*All things are possible to him that believeth*" (Mark 9:23). Since obedience is an act of faith, all things are possible to him who obeys in faith believing. This is important because, although God will never command you to do anything contrary to His Word, He will often command things contrary to your personality, your cultural upbringing and traditions, or even your natural abilities.

It is very easy for those without a personal relationship with God or those with a critical spirit to misunderstand our obedience. They will begin to think that they are justified in saying like Peter, "Not so, Lord!" while condemning those who *did so!* Regardless, we must obey!

Here in Isaiah 45, our Creator is making this case for unquestionable obedience because He's about to ask us to do something that's unthinkable.

Regardless of what it is, we *must obey!* How many of you will obey the Lord? Say it out loud: "Lord God, You are my Maker and whatever You tell me to do, I *will* obey!" Here is what God is commanding us to do: *"Command ye me"* (Isa. 45:11).

There are those who would say, "Not so, Lord. It's blasphemous to even presume to command God." It would be, if He hadn't commanded us to do so. However, with this command, it would be blasphemous *not* to obey it. *He has commanded us to command Him!* To command God is an expression of the highest relationship, friendship, and cooperation.

The "Hand of the King" is a position appointed by royal decree to one who executes the king's commands, with all the kings' resources at their disposal. This person doesn't command the king himself to do anything, but rather can command all things at the king's hand. We saw this in the life of Joseph when he was given authority over Egypt due to the trust he had built with Pharaoh (see Gen. 41:41). Here are some additional examples:

- Moses commanded the hand of God in judgment against the Egyptians (Exod. 14:27).

- Later, he even spared Israel with his authority in the spirit and caused God to repent (Exod. 32:14).

- Joshua commanded the sun to stand still (Josh. 10).

- Elijah commanded fire from Heaven (2 Kings 1:10).

- Jesus commanded the wind and the waves (Mark 4:39).

- The disciples and others commanded men to be free from infirmity (Acts 3:6).

You have been given a weapon that wields divine authority. It's time to use it and not abuse it. We cannot command God with a limited acquaintance with Him. We must all go to God and get a word from Him. We must see that we are right with God. We must grow in understanding and oneness with Him in His work. Without that, we cannot command God.

How do we command the hand of God? That's why we've been given the name of Jesus. When we pray in that name, we are commanding the hand of God. When we pray underneath the canopy of that authority, we are accessing all the power that is at the right hand of God.

What have you been petitioning Heaven for that God has given you the authority to command?

In 1885, the rattling of the world's first automatic machine gun could be heard as its inventor Hiram S. Maxim harnessed the energy released in a firing cartridge. The nature of warfare changed in that moment as this new weapon came on the scene and dominated the battlefield. So it will be when the church begins to fire off rapid prayers of authority in the spirit. The enemy will flee in terror!

This is the time of the supernatural intervention of God into the natural affairs of men:

- Jesus is seated at the right hand of God (Mark 16:19).

- He has given authority to us as believers (Matt. 28:18-20).

- He has seated us with Christ in heavenly places (Eph. 2:6).

We have entered into the dispensation of the Church; it is time to retrieve our spiritual weapons from the house of the Lord, recognize the authority we have in Christ, and move forward with boldness in Christ.

Notes

1. Gurnall, *The Christian in Compleat Armour.*
2. William De Arteaga, "The 'Happy Hunter's' Revolution in Healing Prayer," *Pentecostal Theology,* October 12, 2019, https://www.pentecostaltheology.com/the -happy-hunters-revolution-in-healing-prayer.

CHAPTER SIX

THE AVENGING PRAYER

And from the days of John the Baptist until the present time, the kingdom of heaven has endured violent assault, and violent men seize it by force [as a precious prize—a share in the heavenly kingdom is sought with most ardent zeal and intense exertion].
—MATTHEW 11:12 AMPC

"Don't get mad, get even."

Big government had managed to seize the reins of power. Their iron fist of control over the media and educational institutions had solidified. All prominent dissenting voices had been silenced. Communism was the gospel of the government and atheism blanketed the land.

This may sound eerily similar to what we're facing today, but these were the conditions in China in the 1920s. Hatred and intolerance for Christianity had gone beyond discussion, and there was righteous blood in the streets.

Every nation and generation has a specific yoke—fashioned by satan—to bind them and blind them to the Gospel, but for every yoke of the enemy, God has an anointing.

It is as true today as it was then. Amid the turmoil in China, and in answer to believing prayer, God raised up an unyielding voice whose words would travel to meet us a century later, unobstructed by time. His name was Watchman Nee.

After a radical conversion at the age of 17, Nee embraced a new Chinese name meaning "the sound of the watchman's rattle." Oh, how his words still rattle the soul of all those who read the astonishing revelations God gave him for the church.

Nee had a brilliant mind. He was able to quickly absorb and assimilate the writings of great generals like Andrew Murray, T. Austin Sparks, John Bunyan, George Muller, Hudson Taylor and others. His own writings—*Spiritual Authority, The Breaking of the Outer Man,* and *The Normal Christian Life*—stand to this day without equal. The insightfulness and poignancy of his writings was not a recycled truth borrowed from someone else's experience; it was a realized truth born from real pain and persecution.

We rarely recognize greatness when it is among us. Sadly, much of Watchman Nee's struggle came from the brethren. As he railed against the shallow denominational divisions in the church, he was ostracized by those who should have embraced him.

Americans often idealize persecution as a panacea for all their collective church woes. They offer such sentiments as: "When the American church is really persecuted, *then* we'll come together."

The problem is that pettiness knows no bounds. I've personally worked with persecuted believers around the globe, and I can tell you that the same divisions that haunt the western church are endemic all over the world.

Watchman Nee stood when no one stood with him. Alone and in destitute poverty, he allowed himself to be a weapon in the hands of God. For years, he preached and raised up churches until his arrest in 1952. After more than 15 years in jail, having been allowed only one visitor and suffering with severe physical ailments, he refused to deny his faith. In 1972, while still in captivity, he left these earthly bonds and received his eternal reward in Heaven.

I am sharing this with you because I want you to know where the revelation you are about to receive came from. What you're about to discover is not something concocted in the ivory towers of some theological seminary or blithely penned by a televangelist's ghostwriter. This was born in the crucible of conflict, and it will only yield its treasures to those who understand its origin and are willing to leverage it only for the glory of Christ's eternal Kingdom.

Long Forgotten; Now Remembered

There is a prayer, long forgotten, that is a weapon of precision and power in the right hands. In his book titled *Let Us Pray*,[1] we have a treasure trove of gems mined out for us by Watchman Nee. There is, however, one particular revelation on prayer that I believe is prophetic for where we are today. His message was titled "Prayer that Resists Satan." The Lord shared some things with me from this message that we will now unpack together:

> *And he spake a parable unto them to this end, that men ought always to pray, and not to faint; saying, There was in a city a judge, which feared not God, neither regarded man: and there was a widow in that city; and she came unto him, saying, Avenge me of mine adversary. And he would not for a while: but afterward he said within himself, Though I fear not God, nor regard man; yet because this widow troubleth me, I will avenge her, lest by her continual coming she weary me. And the Lord said, Hear what the unjust judge saith. And shall not God avenge his own elect, which cry day and night unto him, though he bear long with them? I tell you that he will avenge them speedily. Nevertheless when the Son of man cometh, shall he find faith on the earth?* (Luke 18:1-8)

This parable illustrates that there is a certain kind of prayer that has been almost entirely neglected in the church. This negligence has allowed the enemy to take possession of way too much real estate in our lives. It's been said that evil can only triumph when good men do nothing, but it can also triumph when good folks are unaware of legal loopholes. I believe that when we stand before God in eternity, we will be appalled by how much the enemy has gotten away with, mostly due to our ignorance of God's available power.

As we sift through this parable to discover the prophetic gold hidden therein, it is important to remember the context. Jesus had been discussing the last days and comparing them to the days of Noah (see Luke 17:26-37). He had been preaching to His disciples about the importance of prevailing faith. As He diagnosed the faithless nature of this world in the last days, He goes on to give us the antidote:

> *Men ought always to pray, and not to faint* (Luke 18:1).

In difficult times, men will either pray or they will faint. There is no alternative. If you are praying, you will not be fainting. If you are fainting, it is a sign that you are not praying.

During World War II when the bombing of London was so intense, a sign appeared in the front of one of the churches there that read, "If your knees knock together, kneel on them." In times of difficulty and darkness, a fleeting memory of God or His Word cannot light the way. Only consistent, vibrant, up-to-date communion with the divine will suffice.

The kind of relevant prayer that Jesus is talking about here communicates on three dimensions. Persistent prayer that pushes through perilous times must speak to and be aware of three different kingdoms. Watchman Nee discusses these kingdoms in his book—but allow me to distill it for you.

The first kingdom is the one in which we live. In this, our prayers speak to our own personal needs. The third kingdom is the one in which God lives, and this speaks to the advancement of His Kingdom. But there is a second kingdom often ignored by the church that stands between the other two. The second kingdom is that of our adversary, the devil. End-time prayer warriors must learn to speak to this kingdom as well, if they wish to avoid "fainting." This is where Jesus places much of His focus in this parable.

How many times have we seen a sincere believer who is seeking the glory of Christ and who is declaring the Word of God over their lives faint, burn out, or give up along the way? How is this possible? It is possible because satan has wearied them because they did not pray in a way that would influence the second kingdom.

When we read the parable of the unjust judge, we learn a lot about the judge and the widow. We learn that this judge and his response to the widow is a parable in contrast. He is not a reflection of God. He reflects everything God is not. This man is unjust, and yet even he is willing to respond to this widow's cry because of her persistence. How much more will the just and righteous Judge of Heaven respond to us when we pray?

It truly is a thrilling lesson! Your God is a prayer-answering God. Your God will avenge you speedily because He loves you—and your request is just. That's great, but there's more.

So far, we have only looked at two of the three kingdoms represented—that of the widow, and that of the judge. What about the adversary?

The importance of this character in the story cannot be overstated. Some might suggest, and with good cause, that the antagonist is the central figure of this narrative. Without the enemy, there would be no parable!

> *Be sober, be vigilant; because your adversary the devil, as a roaring lion, walketh about, seeking whom he may devour* (1 Peter 5:8).

I know that you have suffered at the hands of the enemy. He has attacked your family, your health, and your confidence in God. He uses a myriad of problems and people to persecute you and wear you down. He tries to rob you of your peace and security in Christ, but I want you to know that his days are numbered in your life.

Watchman Nee, with all his experience and insight, believed that one of the biggest weaknesses a Christian can have is not hating the devil enough. We allow our adversary to get away with too much! We've become way too accustomed to his evil operation in our lives and it's time to get mad.

We shouldn't say, "Oh well, it's just another attack of the devil." No! If we wish to operate in a new dimension of prayer, we must mark every trespass, remember every violation of our person, and note every attack on our homes. Why? So that we can bring it before the Righteous Judge!

There is no comparison between the power of our enemy and the power of our God. Our God is the supreme judge of the universe, but no matter how powerful a judge is, He cannot rule on a case that has not been brought before Him.

The widow represents one who is utterly alone because her husband has left this world. What a picture of the church! Her adversary has tried to take advantage of her condition. Not much is said in her summary to the judge in this parable, but these five words represent the bulk of the communication going on in this scenario: "*Avenge me of mine adversary.*" This end-time prayer is what I call the Avenging Prayer!

We often silence the rising righteous indignation in our hearts and stifle this power-filled prayer by quoting Romans 12:19 out of context. Let's take a look at it:

> *Dearly beloved, avenge not yourselves, but rather give place unto wrath: for it is written, Vengeance is mine; I will repay, saith the Lord.*

The reckless assumption is that we have no business even thinking about vengeance and so we should just close our mouths and leave it in the hands of God. Nothing could be further from the truth! God is not telling us to keep from seeking vengeance. He is telling us to keep from taking vengeance into our own hands. We should seek vengeance, but we should seek it from Heaven. The implication is that if justice is not sought, justice can be delayed.

How have you been attacked by the devil this week? Have you been victimized by his evil plans at all this year? It is outrageous that he would ever dare to attack a child of God, but even more disgraceful is the child of God who says nothing in response to his torments. When was the last time you pleaded for justice against your enemy?

This is one of the primary points of the parable: Don't stop seeking vengeance from Heaven against your adversary! Vengeance is promised to those who persistently seek it.

Are you ready to see God make your spiritual enemy pay for what he's done to you? Patient petitions are the key to seeing divine vengeance.

Hold Not Thy Peace

What does a prayer for vengeance look like? It begins with the simple knowledge that God wants to hear from you. I encourage you to read the following verses aloud during your prayer time with your heavenly Father, the Judge:

> *Hold not thy peace, O God of my praise; for the mouth of the wicked and the mouth of the deceitful are opened against me: they have spoken against me with a lying tongue.*
>
> *...Help me, O Lord my God: O save me according to thy mercy: that they may know that this is thy hand; that thou, Lord, hast done it. Let them curse, but bless thou: when they arise, let them be ashamed; but let thy servant rejoice. Let mine adversaries be clothed with shame, and let them cover themselves with their own confusion, as with a mantle. I will greatly praise the Lord with my mouth; yea, I will praise him among the multitude. For he shall stand at the right hand of the poor, to save him from those that condemn his soul* (Psalm 109:1-2, 26-31).

You can almost feel the vindication of God rising as you speak these words aloud. The avenging prayer is not uncommon in scripture. For example, David prayed it often (see Ps. 35, 58, 139). Jeremiah used it as well (see Jer. 15:15-18).

How does this translate into the New Testament where we are commanded to "love our enemies" (see Matt. 5:44)? In the Old Testament, these were prayers against other individuals. In the New Testament, these are prayers against principalities and powers:

> *Let their table become a snare before them: and that which should have been for their welfare, let it become a trap. Let their eyes be darkened, that they see not; and make their loins continually to shake. Pour out thine indignation upon them, and let thy wrathful anger take hold of them* (Psalm 69:22-24).

As you embrace this new and radical form of spiritual warfare, I believe that God is going to send confusion into the camp of your enemy (see 2 Chron. 20).

> *I will send my fear before thee, and will destroy all the people to whom thou shalt come, and I will make all thine enemies turn their backs unto thee* (Exodus 23:27).

It is possible to love our enemies while praying for judgment on our spiritual foe at the same time. There is no condemnation in this kind of prayer when our hearts are in the right place.

How often and how long should we pray for the vengeance of God to fall on our adversary? Allow me to answer that question with another question: how often and how long does the enemy attack you? The answer to both is—every day! We should not cease to wield this weapon until we meet Jesus in the clouds of glory and His enemies are made His footstool (see Heb. 10:13).

This kind of warfare praying is not intimidated by time. It is neither fearful of repetition nor apprehensive about going too long. This is the purpose of the parable: *"Men ought always to pray."*

According to Watchman Nee, this avenging prayer should not just be extended in times of perceived need, but it should be offered without rest. He suggests that we should accuse our adversary incessantly because this is how often he accuses us. This prayer demands reparations. This prayer brings satan before the throne of God to give an account for his misdeeds. Satan is known as *"the accuser of our brethren...which accused them before our God day and night"* (Rev. 12:10). Recognizing the enemy's *modus operandi*, the avenging prayer launches an always-appropriate countersuit.

Is it possible that our accusations can allow God to restrict satan's movement in our lives? God has chosen not to act alone. He wants to participate with us in the glory of His victory over satan. All we must do is pray the very same prayers that David or Jeremiah prayed—with persistence against our enemy and jubilant faith in our God—and we will find ourselves cooperating with His divine vengeance.

This persistent prayer is so potent that the will of the judge is portrayed as irrelevant in this parable. Mediate on that for a minute! When understood, this has almost frightening implications.

Now, instead of focusing on getting our prayers answered, we must focus on the nature of our prayer. Is our prayer in line with God's perfect will?

The children of Israel prayed for a king. It was not God's will for them to be ruled by any king other than Himself. The Bible says that the answer to their prayer *"sent leanness into their soul"* (Ps. 106:15). What a radically different paradigm! We should be careful what we ask for because our God hears and answers persistent prayer.

This is not to say that God will give us whatever we "pester" Him for, but it should change how we look at His faithfulness to answer when we call on Him. This kind of prayer requires a higher level of maturity and knowledge of God's Word.

Jesus concluded this parable in Luke 18:8 by saying, *"Nevertheless when the Son of man cometh, shall he find faith on the earth?"* Is Jesus telling us that in the last days there will be a lack of this kind of vengeance-seeking faith in the earth? Will He find it in your church? Will He find this weapon in your hand?

We are not only given the authority to bind the enemy (see Matt. 16:18-19); it is also our right to accuse him before the throne of God and receive just compensation. Proverbs 6:31 says, *"But if he be found, he shall restore sevenfold; he shall give all the substance of his house."*

The word *found* implies his capture as well as his court case. Sevenfold restoration will not take place without a proper hearing before the Righteous Judge.

Have we been heard today or has this faith been absent from our homes? It's time to become intentional about making our opposition toward satan known in prayer. This "avenging prayer" and the knowledge that God has heard it will keep us from fainting in battle in these last days.

The Spear of Phineas

Throughout Israel's long history of rebellion and repentance runs a common theme—deliverance. No matter what situation the Israelites found themselves in, a deliverer always came on the scene to right what was wrong, someone who would avenge God's people and not faint when confronted by the enemy.

This was both a continual foreshadowing of the Deliverer who was to come and an ongoing demonstration of God's desire to use ordinary people to accomplish great things.

There was a man named Phineas, the son of the priest Eleazar and grandson of Aaron the high priest. No doubt he had heard the stories of Israel's history over and over again growing up in such a family.

During Phineas' lifetime, Israel had once again fallen into sin and rebellion against God. This time, the sin was immorality and idolatry—entering into intimate relationships with the very people God had told them to avoid, and turning their back on the true God to worship the pagan gods of the Moabites.

And Israel abode in Shittim, and the people began to commit whoredom with the daughters of Moab. And they called the people unto the sacrifices of their gods: and the people did eat, and bowed down to their gods. And Israel joined himself unto Baalpeor: and the anger of the Lord was kindled against Israel (Numbers 25:1-3).

Because of their sin, a plague was running through the camp, and they knew that God was displeased with them. As they gathered together to pray for the sins of their nation, an Israelite man brought one of the foreign women into the camp and into his tent in full view of the people. Phineas saw this and responded immediately:

And when Phinehas, the son of Eleazar, the son of Aaron the priest, saw it, he rose up from among the congregation, and took a javelin in his hand; and he went after the man of Israel into the tent, and thrust both of them through, the man of Israel, and the woman through her belly. So the plague was stayed from the children of Israel (Numbers 25:7-8).

I realize that today, in the church age (because Jesus took upon Himself the full penalty for sin), we are no longer called upon to take up a sword and run our enemies through. However, we are called upon to take up the sword of the Spirit—the Word of God—and use it against the evils we face in our day.

Verses 12 and 13 give God's response to Phineas:

Wherefore say, Behold, I give unto him my cove-
nant of peace: and he shall have it, and his seed after
him, even the covenant of an everlasting priesthood;
because he was zealous for his God, and made an
atonement for the children of Israel.

Does this describe you? Will it be written of you that you were zealous for your God? Will it be said of you that God was able to use you to accomplish great things in His Kingdom?

Phineas used a natural spear against the ones who had defied the true and living God. By his actions, he avenged Israel, and the plague was stayed. We have a spiritual sword—the Word of God—which we are to use against the enemy of our souls.

The sword of Phineas became an avenging weapon against idolatry in his hand. The sword of the Spirit—speaking the Word of God into a situation—becomes an avenging weapon in our arsenal against the idolatry of our age.

For his actions, Phineas was granted an everlasting covenant of peace. Does this sound familiar? We, also, have entered into an everlasting *"covenant of peace"* (Ezek. 34:25) with the Lord Jesus Christ. God has promised to bless us with peace and prosperity as we serve Him.

Let them shout for joy, and be glad, that favour my
righteous cause: yea, let them say continually, Let
the Lord be magnified, which hath pleasure in the
prosperity of his servant. And my tongue shall speak
of thy righteousness and of thy praise all the day long
(Psalm 35:27-28).

I want you to take a moment right now to consider three or four things the enemy has used to negatively impact your life. Think of any ways in which you, or those you love, have suffered loss as a result of satan's attacks. Write them down on a piece of paper and place them by the 35th Psalm in your Bible.

Once you've done that, take them before the throne of God by personalizing this prayer offered by David:

> *Plead my cause, O Lord, with them that strive with me: fight against them that fight against me. Take hold of shield and buckler, and stand up for mine help. Draw out also the spear, and stop the way against them that persecute me: say unto my soul, I am thy salvation. Let them be confounded and put to shame that seek after my soul: let them be turned back and brought to confusion that devise my hurt. Let them be as chaff before the wind: and let the angel of the Lord chase them. Let their way be dark and slippery: and let the angel of the Lord persecute them* (Psalm 35:1-6).

Now know that your God has heard and will answer you speedily! Know it! Allow that knowledge to put steel in your nerves. Allow that knowledge to keep you from fainting when everything else within you wants to give up. Speak the Word of God into every situation that rises up against you that is contrary to the Word of God. Your God will hear you, and He will avenge you!

> *And the God of peace shall bruise Satan under your feet shortly. The grace of our Lord Jesus Christ be with you. Amen* (Romans 16:20).

Note

1. Watchman Nee, *Let Us Pray* (New York: Christian Fellowship Publishers, 1977).

CHAPTER SEVEN

MILITANT WORSHIP

And when they began to sing and to praise, the Lord set ambushments against the children of Ammon, Moab, and mount Seir, which were come against Judah; and they were smitten.

—2 CHRONICLES 20:22

"We had a nice little army until this war came along and mussed up everything."

—WILLIAM SEAVER WOODS[1]

As modern technology makes the world smaller and smaller, it becomes increasingly possible for a single act of violence to instigate a global conflict. World War I is often said to have begun with a single act (the assassination of Archduke Ferdinand of Austria), which led to more than sixteen million deaths in countries around the world. A conflict that started in one nation resulted in worldwide casualties.

Biblically, the spiritual battle we find ourselves in began when lucifer led one-third of the angels in rebellion against God. Since then, this conflict has spilled over into our daily lives and affects everyone, all over the world.

The devil has been temping people to reject God since the Garden of Eden. In this war, there are just two sides—God and satan. When we accept Jesus Christ as our Lord and Savior, we are declaring war against the kingdom of darkness.

> *For we are not fighting against people made of flesh and blood, but against persons without bodies—the evil rulers of the unseen world, those mighty satanic beings and great evil princes of darkness who rule this world; and against huge numbers of wicked spirits in the spirit world* (Ephesians 6:12 TLB).

When we're born again, we are born into war. Everything we do must be tinged with a hint of spiritual violence because we're always operating against adversarial forces. The word *against* in Ephesians 6:12 indicates proximity. It's the same Greek word that's used for *with* in John 1:1 to describe how close the Word is to God:

> *In the beginning was the Word, and the Word was with God, and the Word was God* (emphasis added).

That's how close we are to principalities and powers that desire our destruction. They do not sleep; night and day they are working their dastardly schemes to wipe the name of God off the earth. They want nothing more than to rob the earth of everything that reflects the glory of God. They are always refining their weapons and tailoring their plans to keep each generation out of the presence of God. Is the church keeping pace in this spiritual space race? The battle is to stay in the presence of God, despite the attacks of the adversary.

The first war in the Bible is found in Genesis 14:1–17 as it describes War of the Nine Kings. Abraham's nephew Lot and his family were seized by the enemy. When Abram heard that his nephew had been taken captive, he called out the 318 trained men born in his household and went in pursuit (see Gen. 14:14). He recovered all the goods and brought back Lot and his possessions, together with the women and the other people at the end of the story. He was victorious, but it required lots of resources, energy, and skill.

> *And when Abram heard that his brother was taken captive, he armed his trained servants, born in his own house, three hundred and eighteen, and pursued them unto Dan* (Genesis 14:14).

I want you to look at this verse alongside First Corinthians 10:11:

> *Now all these things happened unto them for ensamples: and they are written for our admonition, upon whom the ends of the world are come.*

Abraham, the father of our faith and our example, had 318 trained men in his house, and he armed them all. That's what's happening to you right now. God is arming you for victory. In the very first war mentioned in the Bible, we see that God's people were already well trained and well equipped. Too often, though, we are completely unprepared for the attacks that come against us. I believe that God is training and arming His church for a conflict yet to be seen. We must be ready!

A passive church will seek shelter from the battle at all costs. They'll compromise and take the weapons God has given us for battle and turn them into maintenance tools. The Bible says that there will come a day when we will beat our swords into plowshares and our spears into pruning hooks and *"neither shall they learn war anymore"* (Isa. 2:4). But—we're not there yet! We've jumped the gun on this prophecy. Churches are taking the deadly weapons of the Spirit and using them to maintain the gardens of their church.

The Word of God is a sword, not a shovel. Worship is a weapon, not a church growth strategy. We've prematurely turned the deadliest arsenal on the planet into a hippie commune. It's time to beat these plowshares back into swords. It's time to take the weapons we've been using for maintenance and turn them back into machines of war. It's time for us to be trained to fight for the glory. Are we ready to modernize our weapons?

Weapon Modernization

If we are not properly trained and equipped, victory in this battle will be impossible. In the 19th century, there was an uprising that occurred in the wake of the Meiji Restoration in

Japan. It was during this time that Japan began to implement modernization in terms of weapons in its military. The samurai warriors, historically the elite class of warriors trained to protect Japan, objected to this transformation:

> The Meiji Restoration of 1868 signaled the beginning of the end for Japan's samurai warriors. After centuries of samurai rule, however, many members of the warrior class were understandably reluctant to give up their status and power. They also believed that only the samurai had the courage and training to defend Japan from its enemies, internal and external. Surely no conscript army of peasants could fight like the Samurai! In 1877, the samurai of the Satsuma Province rose up in the Satsuma Rebellion or Seinan Senso (Southwestern War), challenging the authority of the Restoration Government in Tokyo and testing the new imperial army.[2]

The samurai engaged in fierce battles against the Japanese Imperial Army in order to preserve their traditions, but they refused to modernize their weapons. They believed that the samurai himself was the greatest weapon. Honorable as this may sound, it didn't stand up well against rifles, cannons, and Gatling guns. The samurai warriors had only their traditional weaponry while the Japanese Empire had a full array of modern weapons at their disposal.

While I admire their courage and bravery, the samurai were no match for the modernized army. They lost the battle to preserve their traditions, and they slowly disappeared.

Traditions should be honored and respected for the place they hold in history, but there comes a time we must move on. This is true in the spirit realm as well as in the natural realm.

Spiritual warfare is just as deadly, if not more so, than natural warfare because the stakes are eternal. Both believers and non-believers become casualties in this battle. Satan's goal is to seal, kill, and destroy (see John 10:10). We are "against" these forces every moment of every day:

> *Be very careful, then, how you live—not as unwise*
> *but as wise, making the most of every opportunity,*
> *because the days are evil* (Ephesians 5:15-16 NIV).

Are we making the most of every opportunity? I'm going to show you a particular "plowshare" that we use every week that needs to be turned back into a weapon of war—worship.

Warring for the Glory

We are warring for the glory of God, to preserve the presence of God in our midst. Satan wants to keep us out of the presence of God. It is no wonder that he continually tries to block us from connecting with God—in God's presence is fullness of joy, and the joy of the Lord is our strength (see Ps. 16:11; Neh. 8:10). Our enemy does not want us to be strong, rather the opposite. He wants to keep us weak and ineffective against him.

If we look back over our lives, we will see the many times we attempted to get into the presence of God only to have our phones ring, our kids scream, or something just come up out of the blue that needed to be taken care of. The enemy is trying to keep us from the glory of God.

> *But thou art holy, O thou that inhabitest the praises of Israel* (Psalm 22:3).

If the presence of God is our priority, then worship must be our priority. Praise invokes the presence of God; worship increases the square footage that God is able to inhabit in our lives. We can literally increase the borders of God's habitation in the earth through worship. I know that there are many nuances between the terms *praise* and *worship*, but for our purposes we will be using them interchangeably in this chapter.

It's time to modernize the weapon of our worship. Let me define what I mean by that. I don't mean that we need, as my friend Mario Murillo says, "Big screens, skinny jeans, and fog machines."[3] When I say *modernize*, I simply mean to take it back to the biblical model so that it can be effective in our modern day. Today's over-organized, entertainment-driven worship has little resemblance to what we see in the Word of God. Worship is a weapon.

When Jehoshaphat was King of Judah, an array of armies came up against him. Read this account of how worship affected the outcome this battle:

> *Ye shall not need to fight in this battle: set your-selves, stand ye still, and see the salvation of the Lord with you, O Judah and Jerusalem: fear not, nor be dismayed; to morrow go out against them: for the Lord will be with you.*

And Jehoshaphat bowed his head with his face to the ground: and all Judah and the inhabitants of Jerusalem fell before the Lord, worshipping the Lord. And the Levites, of the children of the Kohathites, and of the children of the Korhites, stood up to praise the Lord God of Israel with a loud voice on high.

And they rose early in the morning, and went forth into the wilderness of Tekoa: and as they went forth, Jehoshaphat stood and said, Hear me, O Judah, and ye inhabitants of Jerusalem; Believe in the Lord your God, so shall ye be established; believe his prophets, so shall ye prosper.

And when he had consulted with the people, he appointed singers unto the Lord, and that should praise the beauty of holiness, as they went out before the army, and to say, Praise the Lord; for his mercy endureth for ever.

And when they began to sing and to praise, the Lord set ambushments against the children of Ammon, Moab, and mount Seir, which were come against Judah; and they were smitten. For the children of Ammon and Moab stood up against the inhabitants of mount Seir, utterly to slay and destroy them: and when they had made an end of the inhabitants of Seir, every one helped to destroy another.

And when Judah came toward the watch tower in the wilderness, they looked unto the multitude, and, behold, they were dead bodies fallen to the earth, and none escaped (2 Chronicles 20:17-24).

Jehoshaphat and his army had a word from God: send the singers and praisers out ahead of the army. This might seem backward to us—shouldn't the rejoicing come after the battle has been won? But they obeyed, and God worked miraculously on their behalf. Their enemies turned on themselves and destroyed each other.

The enemy will do whatever he can to keep us from this kind of worship. This is why, in these last days, our worship must always have a hint of violence behind it: *"the kingdom of heaven suffereth violence, and the violent take it by force"* (Matt. 11:12). Why? Because there's always something or someone trying to keep us from it. I call this renewed revelation *militant worship*.

Militant Worship

One night, I was teaching a Bible lesson to a small group. Have you ever been in a moment when you could sense the presence of God in the atmosphere, and you knew something was about to happen? This was not one of those times!

It was a very casual and jovial atmosphere. I had walked out among the crowd and was telling some fun stories about Dr. Lester Sumrall's journeys around the world. As I turned to walk back to the podium, the weighty Spirit of God dropped on me. This was probably the most intense encounter I have ever experienced with the presence of God. Before I could take the next step, I crumbled to the floor and began to weep uncontrollably. I didn't know what was happening, and frankly, I was embarrassed.

I tried to pick myself up, but the weight was so heavy that I could barely lift my head up off the ground. I managed to crawl up the steps of the platform, and then finally collapsed behind the pulpit. I didn't know how long I was there or what the crowd was doing during that time. All I remember were the intense wailings that came up out of my spirit that night.

After an unknown period of time, I was able to collect myself and stagger into a room behind the stage. The moment I closed the door behind me, it hit me again. An intercessory prayer began to flow in torrents from my innermost being. That night the Spirit of God prayed through me so intensely that capillaries in my eyes burst. My eyes looked like they were filled with blood for some time afterward.

I asked God what had happened to me. He spoke to me and said, "I'm imparting a warring spirit and a militant worship that will overthrow My enemies." He then proceeded to give me five words that describe what this worship looks like:

- Zealous
- Forceful
- Vigorous
- Combative
- Disturbing

Militant worship isn't like regular worship that passively and peaceably seeks God during a slow song. When we enter into militant worship, we are zealously, forcefully, vigorously, combatively, and disturbingly seeking God, because there are external forces and internal conflicts that aspire to keep us out of His presence. Real victory takes place when we remain in His presence. That's the battle. Once we get in the glory, the Lord fights on our behalf. So, the real struggle is to stay in the glory.

There are forces all around us, 24 hours a day, that are trying to keep us out of the glory of God. If we know that this is true, why do we worship as if it's not? We ignore the reality of the conflict and, as a result, rarely break through into the presence of God.

Worship with Whips

Jesus wasn't content to allow anything to keep people from God's presence, and He got militant about it:

> *And found in the temple those that sold oxen and sheep and doves, and the changers of money sitting: and when he had made a scourge of small cords, he drove them all out of the temple, and the sheep, and the oxen; and poured out the changers' money, and overthrew the tables; and said unto them that sold doves, Take these things hence; make not my Father's house an house of merchandise. And his disciples remembered that it was written, The zeal of thine house hath eaten me up* (John 2:14-17).

The problem was not simply that they were buying and selling. Many merchants were performing a noble service by providing travelers who came long distances with the ability to purchase sacrifices that would have been too difficult to bring with them.

It was not just the dishonesty of many of these sellers. These merchants had taken up the only space that the Gentiles were allowed to use to come and worship at the temple. They were in the way of worship. They were keeping people from invoking the presence of God.

What was Jesus' response? He took time to fashion a homemade whip and proceeded to increase the borders of God's habitation.

If God's house is to be a house of prayer, we must worship with whips when it is a den of thieves. This kind of worship is eaten up with a zeal that cannot be quenched. Those who have broken through to receive from God or do great exploits for Him did so with a militancy that is almost nonexistent in today's church.

We think that we can get it on our own terms. We say, "God knows my heart." Yes, God knows that our hearts are deceitfully wicked (see Jer. 17:9). I'm glad that blind Bartimaeus didn't lazily hope that God knew his heart. The Bible says that he cried out:

> *And they came to Jericho: and as he went out of Jericho with his disciples and a great number of people, blind Bartimaeus, the son of Timaeus, sat by the highway side begging. And when he heard that it was Jesus of Nazareth, he began to cry out, and say, Jesus, thou son of David, have mercy on me. And many charged him that he should hold his peace: but he cried the more a great deal, Thou son of David, have mercy on me.*

And Jesus stood still, and commanded him to be called. And they call the blind man, saying unto him, Be of good comfort, rise; he calleth thee. And he, casting away his garment, rose, and came to Jesus. And Jesus answered and said unto him, What wilt thou that I should do unto thee? The blind man said unto him, Lord, that I might receive my sight. And Jesus said unto him, Go thy way; thy faith hath made thee whole. And immediately he received his sight, and followed Jesus in the way (Mark 10:46-52).

Did Bartimaeus quickly lift his hands on the 42nd row, hoping for a miracle, or did he seek God...

- Zealously?
- Forcefully?
- Vigorously?
- Combatively?
- Disturbingly?

In fact, when the disciples tried to silence him, he just got more militant in his worship. If you think that Bartimaeus ignoring the direction of the disciples is bold, you ought to look back at what that Syrophoenician woman did in Matthew 15. She argues with God! What's even more stunning is that Jesus called this militant worship "great faith."

And, behold, a woman of Canaan came out of the same coasts, and cried unto him, saying, Have mercy on me, O Lord, thou son of David; my daughter is grievously vexed with a devil. But he answered her not a word. And his disciples came and besought him, saying, Send her away; for she crieth after us. But he answered and said, I am not sent but unto the lost sheep of the house of Israel.

Then came she and worshipped him, saying, Lord, help me. But he answered and said, It is not meet to take the children's bread, and to cast it to dogs. And she said, Truth, Lord: yet the dogs eat of the crumbs which fall from their masters' table. Then Jesus answered and said unto her, O woman, great is thy faith: be it unto thee even as thou wilt. And her daughter was made whole from that very hour (Matthew 15:22-28).

This woman entered into a kind of worship that refused to take "no" for an answer. Does this surprise us? Would we be offended if we entered into a church full of people who were following Bartimaeus' example and crying out to God without restraint? Would it offend our religious sensibilities? It shouldn't, especially when we realize that the entire nation of Israel is built on this kind of militant worship.

When we think about spiritual warfare, we normally think about wrestling against principalities and powers. Jacob, however, wrestled with God Himself at Bethel. To fully understand this, read the chapter on "The Evolution of Warfare":

And Jacob was left alone; and there wrestled a man with him until the breaking of the day. And when he saw that he prevailed not against him, he touched the hollow of his thigh; and the hollow of Jacob's thigh was out of joint, as he wrestled with him. And he said, Let me go, for the day breaketh. And he said, I will not let thee go, except thou bless me. And he said unto him, What is thy name? And he said, Jacob. And he said, Thy name shall be called no more Jacob, but Israel: for as a prince hast thou power with God and with men, and hast prevailed (Genesis 32:24-28).

That's militant worship. Jacob wrestled with God and received a new name. Israel was the name that he was given, and one of its meanings is "the one who strives with God." The entire nation is named after him. God calls His nation "the God-strivers."

There's a divine admiration toward those who so know His character that they refuse anything contrary to it. I think that sometimes God "answers not a word" because He wants to see if we'll press in (see Matt. 15:23).

Worshipers Must Be Warriors

As I continued to press into this revelation, the Spirit of God showed me eight characteristics of this kind of worship:

1. *Militant worship refuses to regard circumstances or be moved by emotions.* As militant worshipers, we're not waiting for the atmosphere to be just right. We're not waiting until we feel like worshiping. We must realize that even when we don't feel like worshiping, the enemy still feels like attacking us!

2. *Militant worship seeks to encounter Christ amid the assailing attacks from without and the encroaching turmoil within.* Just like Blind Bartimaeus, we will not be silenced by our circumstances or the religious community. Don't get me wrong, everything must be done decently and in order, and we should not be a rebel—but we do need to find a tribe that will break through with us.

3. *Militant worship is born of and works by unadulterated faith.* Faith without works is dead (see James 2:14-26). Works without faith are lifeless. This kind of praise cannot be for show. It must exude from a heart of faith that is born out of intimacy with God.

4. *Militant worship unconditionally rejects the suggestion that it can't have the fullness of God right now.* When we begin to walk in this anointing, we will not be satisfied with halfhearted prayers that only take us halfway to our breakthrough. It's all or nothing!

5. *Militant worship requires the unified efforts of the spirit, soul, and body.* The only reason we have a body or emotions is to use them to express praise to God and to display the life He has given us. This kind of worship cannot be fenced in the heart or hidden under a bushel. The body and emotions are led by the spirit into exuberant praise.

6. *Militant worship understands that it's called to move things in the spirit.* There are obstacles that need to be overcome and demonic barriers that must be removed. This worship recognizes its responsibility to actively and intentionally move these things out of the way.

7. *Militant worship seeks to rout the enemy and loot the kingdom of darkness.* Our enemy's plan to steal, kill, and destroy has been uncovered (see John 10:10). Militant worship will not sit casually by and let this happen.

8. *Militant worship will wrestle with anything that gets between them and the promise of God.* Like Jacob of old, militant worship seeks to reclaim that which has been promised. Militant worship opens a portal between this realm and the spirit realm.

It's important to remember that we are born again *into* and live *in* a constant state of war. In His presence, we find peace—but it is a battle, nonetheless. Like the samurai, we must not ignore the evolution of warfare and be overtaken by more advanced or intense weaponry. The enemy is getting more "in your face," open and loud about his kingdom and the church must raise its voice even louder.

The Value of Volume

I can already hear the religious temple guards now. "It doesn't take all that! You don't have to be loud!" How's that working for you? Where's your Great Awakening? I'm not saying that we have to be loud and obnoxious all the time. There is a place for stillness and quiet reverence—but not all reverence is quiet.

The Bible says, *"Be still, and know that I am God,"* but it doesn't say, "Be quiet" (Ps. 46:10)! We can all point to moments when we or some saint of old were confronted with evil and they responded with a quiet but confident, "Come out!" or "Loose them!" with success. But these are the exceptions.

The quiet confidence we wish to exude often only comes from intense seasons of radical warfare. Christians are always trying to find a way out of doing what makes them uncomfortable. "Do I have to do it that way? Can't I just get it by lifting my hands and whispering?"

The truth is that the victory is not in being loud or quiet. The victory is in obedience. We will break through when we obey the Lord and pray like He tells us to pray.

Nearly every act of faith in the New Testament had a hint of violence. From illegally pushing through a crowd to screaming over the disciples and even tearing off a roof, we see what the kind of faith that pleases God looks like (see Mark 5:25-34; Luke 18:39; Mark 2:4). It's disturbing. We want to receive our miracle in secret. Jesus wants to make a show of satan openly. That's why from a practical perspective, spiritual violence nearly always requires volume. We need to lift our voices.

A sound's volume level tells us how loud it is. Volume has three benefits or characteristics that cannot be ignored:

First, confidence is a characteristic that produces volume. When we are certain of something, we lift our voices. When we are unsure, we get quiet. Most justify their timid praise as "just their personality" when usually it's merely a result of them having no confidence in their God, the righteousness He's provided for them, or His Word.

The most confident kid in class is always the loudest. They may annoy everyone else, but they're the ones getting the extra credit. When we're confident in our knowledge of what God has done for us and in the power of our praise, it's hard to keep quiet.

Second, volume affects concentration. Have you ever been driving down the road and said, "Turn that radio down! I'm trying to think!" Why? Because the louder something is, the more difficult it is to think about anything else. Our praise ought to be so loud that it's hard for the devil to get us to think about anything else. This is one of the keys to weaponizing our worship and arming ourselves with praise—increase the volume!

Finally, conquest is always connected to volume. The voice of triumph is the voice of conquest. When the author of this psalm thought of "the voice of triumph," I'm sure he imagined a warrior standing on the defeated corpse of his enemy and screaming at the top of his lungs with a shout that sent terror down the spine of any remaining foe. He had lived this shout and was commanding God's people to keep this conquest shout alive:

O clap your hands, all ye people; shout unto God with the voice of triumph. For the Lord most high is terrible; he is a great King over all the earth (Psalm 47:1-2).

Don't underestimate the value of volume. Sound moves things. Sound is vibration, and our eardrums have been tuned to hear when things vibrate.

We move things with our voices. The louder we get, the more we move. We can use this in our personal prayer time. When we take the volume of our voice higher in prayer than we ever have before, things happen—a whole world of victory opens up to us.

In this crucial hour, the church must learn the value of volume and release a militant worship that clears the house of God of everything that's hindering the glory. We must trample every religious spirit that quenches our faith and attempts to rob of us our volume-lifting confidence (see 1 John 5:14). For those unfamiliar with Jesus, this may seem unchristlike, but we've already seen what Jesus would do in the New Testament. Let's take a look at this militant pursuit of the blessings of God in the Old Testament:

> *Then Elisha said, Hear ye the word of the Lord; Thus saith the Lord, To morrow about this time shall a measure of fine flour be sold for a shekel, and two measures of barley for a shekel, in the gate of Samaria. Then a lord on whose hand the king leaned answered the man of God, and said, Behold, if the Lord would make windows in heaven, might this thing be? And he said, Behold, thou shalt see it with thine eyes, but shalt not eat thereof* (2 Kings 7:1-2).

The city had been besieged by the Syrians and the people of God were starving when the prophet made this prediction. The hand of the king's skepticism was naturally valid, but it was spiritually abhorrent. In desperate times, there's no room for doubt and unbelief. We need to get doubt out of our homes, off our phones, and out of our lives!

Miraculously, God scared the Syrians off, and they ran away so quickly that they left all their food, gold, and possessions behind. When the good news (Gospel) hit the town, the Bible says:

And the people went out, and spoiled the tents of the Syrians. So a measure of fine flour was sold for a shekel, and two measures of barley for a shekel, according to the word of the Lord.

And the king appointed the lord on whose hand he leaned to have the charge of the gate: and the people trode upon him in the gate, and he died, as the man of God had said, who spake when the king came down to him.

And it came to pass as the man of God had spoken to the king, saying, Two measures of barley for a shekel, and a measure of fine flour for a shekel, shall be to morrow about this time in the gate of Samaria: and that lord answered the man of God, and said, Now, behold, if the Lord should make windows in heaven, might such a thing be? And he said, Behold, thou shalt see it with thine eyes, but shalt not eat thereof. And so it fell out unto him: for the people trode upon him in the gate, and he died (2 Kings 7:16-20).

What happened to the doubt-filled religious stick-in-the-mud? He was trampled underneath the feet of those who were passionately pursuing the provision of God. I have an announcement to every professional doubter in the church today: don't get in our way! We'll spiritually climb up over your back and step on your head if you allow the enemy to use you to keep us from the fullness of God. We have a world to win, and we no longer have time to walk on eggshells hoping people won't be offended by our praise.

And from the days of John the Baptist until now the kingdom of heaven suffereth violence, and the violent take it by force (Matthew 11:12).

There is one thing that the Kingdom *suffers* or cannot escape—violence. Until Jesus returns, we will never be able to separate this spiritual militancy from His Kingdom. That means that everything in the Kingdom has a hint of violence to it as well. That includes our worship.

Take this weapon of worship out of the armory of God in your personal prayer time, and then take it into your church. This radical submission to God in worship will terrify your enemy (see James 4:7). This single act of spiritual violence can spark a fire that will spread to the whole world.

Notes

1. William Seaver Woods, *Colossal Blunders of the War* (Montana: Literary Licensing, 2012), 8.

2. Kallie Szczepanski, "The Satsuma Rebellion," ThoughtCo, October 24, 2019. https://www.thoughtco.com/the-satsuma-rebellion-195570.

3. Mario Murillo, "Separate to Me," OpenHeaven.com, October 27, 2019, https://www.openheaven.com/2019/10/27/separate-to-me-mario-murillo.

CHAPTER EIGHT

GOLIATH'S SWORD

And the priest said, The sword of Goliath the Philistine, whom thou slewest in the valley of Elah, behold, it is here wrapped in a cloth behind the ephod: if thou wilt take that, take it: for there is no other save that here. And David said, There is none like that; give it me.

—1 Samuel 21:9

"Many wearing rapiers are afraid of goose-quills and dare scarce come thither."
—WILLIAM SHAKESPEARE, *Hamlet*, Act II, scene ii

Something is happening right now in the Spirit. God is marshalling His forces from every denomination and from every camp within His Body. If you're reading this book, I know you have sensed a shift in the atmosphere. You may not be able to put your finger on it, but you know something big is on the horizon. God is preparing to launch the largest concentration of troops—with the most advanced spiritual weaponry—that the world has ever seen.

As you receive the supernatural wisdom of God, the Holy Spirit is going to take the weapons that the enemy designed to destroy you and use them in your hand to destroy him. God has a reputation for taking what the enemy meant for evil and turning it for good. Although we know this in theory, we're not yet sure how to yield ourselves to it in practice.

Have you been under attack lately? Can you see the hand of satan at work in your family and your nation? It's time for you to learn how to use the enemy's weapons against him.

God used the betrayal of Joseph's brothers to set up the salvation of nations. This is a common theme in the art of God's war:

> *But as for you, ye thought evil against me; but God meant it unto good, to bring to pass, as it is this day, to save much people alive* (Genesis 50:20).

In the book of Esther, we see an evil politician plotting the demise of God's people. All his masterful manipulations simply hastened his own execution. Haman built gallows to hang Mordecai, but before he could conduct the ribbon cutting, he found himself hanging from a short piece of rope. The very weapon he created to destroy God's people was used on him.

> *So they hanged Haman on the gallows that he had prepared for Mordecai. Then was the king's wrath pacified* (Esther 7:10).

Even when we look to the life of our Lord, we see the same *modus operandi*. Satan was constantly agitating the mob and manipulating the leaders in an attempt to kill Jesus. Eventually his masterful plan came to its ultimate end with the most horrendous execution in history.

The cross was created by evil itself as a weapon to silence the voice of salvation. The cross was created to strike fear in the hearts of all who would dare stand against the darkness. Jesus took the weapon of the enemy and turned it against the kingdom of darkness and into a beacon of light and hope for the world.

> *None of the rulers of this age has understood. For if they had understood it, they would not have crucified the Lord of glory* (1 Corinthians 2:8 DLNT).

In modern history, we saw an example of this in the 1930s when Hitler and the Nazis attempted to wipe the Jewish race off the earth. Instead, all he did was awaken the world to the need for a Jewish state. Satan meant to use World War II to destroy the people of God, but instead, that same weapon was used by God to establish the nation of Israel in 1948.

Satan's Weaponry

God has hidden His arsenal for the wise and prudent, but satan's weapons are out in the open for everyone to see (see Matt. 11:25). We don't need to look far. You probably have one of his weapons within your reach right now.

Mankind has never been in this position before. Without having improved appreciably in virtue or enjoying wiser guidance, it has got into its hands for the first time the tools by which it can unfailingly accomplish its own extermination. That is the point in human destinies to which all the glories and toils of men have at last led them. They would do well to pause and ponder upon their new responsibilities.[1]

Winston Churchill was fascinated with technology, but he understood its dangers. The stalemate on the western front during World War I made him seek out new technological revolutions to get the upper hand on the enemy. He believed that the future of war would be won by scientific innovations. He wasn't wrong.

The invention of radar is a prime of example of one of these advances. This, combined with his love for the movie *The Wizard of Oz*, led Churchill to call the Second World War "The Wizard War" behind closed doors. He and one of his closest friends, Frederick Lindemann, would spend countless hours discussing scientific military innovation.

One of the keys to being armed for victory is to know your enemy's weapons and then figure out how to use them against him.

Goliath's Sword

Let's take a step back and look at one of the most pivotal moments in Israel's history. In First Samuel 21, David is on the run from King Saul. Any misstep in this moment will cause the house of David to come to a premature end. There will be no temple, no psalms, and no Messiah if he fails in this conflict. He's discouraged, so he runs to the only place where he can find help—the house of God.

At this time, Ahimelech is the priest in his office, and he's troubled by David's sudden visit. Take a look at how the Bible describes this encounter:

> *Then came David to Nob to Ahimelech the priest: and Ahimelech was afraid at the meeting of David, and said unto him, Why art thou alone, and no man with thee?*
>
> *And David said unto Ahimelech the priest, The king hath commanded me a business, and hath said unto me, Let no man know any thing of the business whereabout I send thee, and what I have commanded thee: and I have appointed my servants to such and such a place.*
>
> *Now therefore what is under thine hand? give me five loaves of bread in mine hand, or what there is present.*
>
> *And the priest answered David, and said, There is no common bread under mine hand, but there is hallowed bread; if the young men have kept them-selves at least from women.*
>
> *And David answered the priest, and said unto him, Of a truth women have been kept from us about these three days, since I came out, and the vessels of the young men are holy, and the bread is in a manner common, yea, though it were sanctified this day in the vessel.*

So the priest gave him hallowed bread: for there was no bread there but the shewbread, that was taken from before the Lord, to put hot bread in the day when it was taken away.

Now a certain man of the servants of Saul was there that day, detained before the Lord; and his name was Doeg, an Edomite, the chiefest of the herdmen that belonged to Saul.

And David said unto Ahimelech, And is there not here under thine hand spear or sword? for I have neither brought my sword nor my weapons with me, because the king's business required haste.

And the priest said, The sword of Goliath the Philistine, whom thou slewest in the valley of Elah, behold, it is here wrapped in a cloth behind the ephod: if thou wilt take that, take it: for there is no other save that here. And David said, There is none like that; give it me (1 Samuel 21:1-9).

Looking back, we see that many (if not all) of the events that involved the nation of Israel were prophetic historical pictures. From the children of Israel's deliverance from Egypt to the conquest of the Promised Land, we see these events as prophetic parallels of what God will accomplish in His church.

The civil war we see in First Samuel 21 between David and Saul is no exception. In fact, I believe it provides us with the perfect picture of what's happening in the church today. The religious house of Saul, which wants to maintain the status quo in the modern church, has launched a coordinated effort to silence the house of David, which will be carriers of the end-time move of God. We can see each character in this story in the modern church today.

Doeg was a chief herdsman of King Saul. His name means "fearful." As a chief herdsman of thousands, he looks to me like a modern mega-church pastor who's more concerned about losing his job security than he is about advancing God's Kingdom. Doeg later betrays the priest and has the entire house of Ahimelech killed for helping David (see 1 Sam. 22:17).

The most tragic figure in this story is the priest, Ahimelech. He and his house were destroyed because he did not know that David and Saul were fighting. He was killed, not because he was *innocent*, but because he was *ignorant*. We have many in the church today who are dying because they are unaware of the battle they are in right now.

Ahimelech just wanted everyone to get along. Ministers who will side with today's woke culture in an attempt to appear loving have no idea that their end will be the same as this priest. It will come back to bite them.

Minsters like these are pawns that God will use to fuel the house of David. We often hear talk about a great end-time wealth transfer from the hands of the wicked into the hands of the righteous—and it's true (see Prov. 13:22). However, I believe that there's also going to be a great transfer from the hands of the so-called-righteous to the called-out remnant.

There are many who have ministries who are not using their resources properly, and God is about to redirect their supplies to those who will. There are buildings, buses, planes, and funds that God is about to slide across the table to those who will be faithful with them.

David's men were hungry, but all there was to eat in the house of God was the sacred bread that was meant only for the priest. God is about to take what's been used for ministry in the house of God and use it to supply His army outside the four walls of the church.

As we see in the story, holiness is a key qualifier. David's men had to have kept themselves clean to partake of the sacred bread. We've had too many ministries fall because they were never taught to avoid the very appearance of evil (see 1 Thess. 5:22-24). It's time for a revival of holiness in God's army. Holiness qualifies us to receive this provisional transfer.

Then we get the best part of this story. David asked the priest if he had any weapons. This may seem like an odd question to us. Why would there be weapons in the house of God? God's desire is to always arm His people for victory. The priest said, "We actually do have a weapon, and you might be familiar with it. We have Goliath's sword."

Remember the history of David's battle with Goliath of Gath? I'm sure you do, but there's more to the story than what we learned in Sunday school.

> *Now the Philistines gathered together their armies to battle, and were gathered together at Shochoh, which belongeth to Judah, and pitched between Shochoh and Azekah, in Ephesdammim. And Saul and the men of Israel were gathered together, and*

pitched by the valley of Elah, and set the battle in array against the Philistines. And the Philistines stood on a mountain on the one side, and Israel stood on a mountain on the other side: and there was a valley between them. And there went out a champion out of the camp of the Philistines, named Goliath, of Gath, whose height was six cubits and a span.

And he had an helmet of brass upon his head, and he was armed with a coat of mail; and the weight of the coat was five thousand shekels of brass. And he had greaves of brass upon his legs, and a target of brass between his shoulders. And the staff of his spear was like a weaver's beam; and his spear's head weighed six hundred shekels of iron: and one bearing a shield went before him.

And he stood and cried unto the armies of Israel, and said unto them, Why are ye come out to set your battle in array? am not I a Philistine, and ye servants to Saul? choose you a man for you, and let him come down to me. If he be able to fight with me, and to kill me, then will we be your servants: but if I prevail against him, and kill him, then shall ye be our servants, and serve us. And the Philistine said, I defy the armies of Israel this day; give me a man, that we may fight together. When Saul and all Israel heard those words of the Philistine, they were dismayed, and greatly afraid (1 Samuel 17:1-11).

Goliath is described as a giant, standing at least ten feet tall. He has a coat of mail that weighs more than 150 pounds. His spear is around eighteen pounds and is like a weaver's beam. A weaver's beam is two and a half inches thick and can extend to twelve feet in length. It's no wonder that King Saul was greatly dismayed. Goliath seemed like an insurmountable foe.

This is the perfect picture of satan, whose grip on this nation and the world seems gigantic. He's taunting us when he locks down churches—but opens abortion clinics. He's taunting us when he encourages protests—but bans praise in church. He's taunting us when he bans Christian voices on the internet—but accelerates the volume of filth available to our children on social media. It seems insurmountable, but what if God is about to take the weapons that the enemy has been using to taunt us and turn them around to destroy him?

What was it that killed Goliath? The religious answer is always the same: the stone from David's sling. Though it certainly played a part, the stone from the sling wasn't what slew Goliath. Let's look at it together:

And David girded his sword upon his armour, and he assayed to go; for he had not proved it. And David said unto Saul, I cannot go with these; for I have not proved them. And David put them off him. And he took his staff in his hand, and chose him five smooth stones out of the brook, and put them in a shepherd's bag which he had, even in a scrip; and his sling was in his hand: and he drew

*near to the Philistine. And the Philistine came on
and drew near unto David; and the man that bare
the shield went before him. And when the Philistine
looked about, and saw David, he disdained him:
for he was but a youth, and ruddy, and of a fair
countenance. And the Philistine said unto David,
Am I a dog, that thou comest to me with staves?
And the Philistine cursed David by his gods. And
the Philistine said to David, Come to me, and I
will give thy flesh unto the fowls of the air, and
to the beasts of the field. Then said David to the
Philistine, Thou comest to me with a sword, and
with a spear, and with a shield: but I come to thee in
the name of the Lord of hosts, the God of the armies
of Israel, whom thou hast defied. This day will the
Lord deliver thee into mine hand; and I will smite
thee, and take thine head from thee; and I will give
the carcases of the host of the Philistines this day
unto the fowls of the air, and to the wild beasts of
the earth; that all the earth may know that there is
a God in Israel. And all this assembly shall know
that the Lord saveth not with sword and spear: for
the battle is the Lord's, and he will give you into
our hands. And it came to pass, when the Philistine
arose, and came, and drew nigh to meet David, that
David hastened, and ran toward the army to meet
the Philistine. And David put his hand in his bag,
and took thence a stone, and slang it, and smote the
Philistine in his forehead, that the stone sunk into*

*his forehead; and he fell upon his face to the earth.
So David prevailed over the Philistine with a sling
and with a stone, and smote the Philistine, and slew
him; but there was no sword in the hand of David.
Therefore David ran, and stood upon the Philistine,
and took his sword, and drew it out of the sheath
thereof, and slew him, and cut off his head there-
with. And when the Philistines saw their champion
was dead, they fled* (1 Samuel 17:39-51).

Did you see it? David finished Goliath off with his own weapon. David used enemy technology. What the enemy was using to intimidate and harm God's people, David turned against him. Taking possession of the enemy's weapons means never allowing them to be used against us or those we love again.

Media today is a mighty weapon, and there are too many Christians who have been intimidated by it or are ignorant of its power. Imagine an entity so powerful that it could program an entire generation to think a certain way. Then, imagine that entity convincing Christians to pay for it!

Parents may give their children a few hours of religious instruction in a seven-day period, while media giants from Hollywood and Silicon Valley spend more than forty hours a week with them through that screen. These propaganda companies aren't just in it for the money. If that were true, they would rate all their movies G or PG. Family-rated media makes two to three times more money than anything R-rated. Even the top grossing R-rated movie was *The Passion of the Christ* for a long time.

They're not making movies with perverse sensuality, gratuitous violence, and vile profanity for the money. The main reason they are doing it is to influence culture. They want society to be as depraved as they are. Most of what we call the news today is just what those who own the news want the country to be talking about.

In the theological study of eschatology, there is much debate over who the false prophet will be during the great tribulation, but I think there's little argument over who is possessed by this spirit today—the media.

In response, the church generally reacts in one of two ways. Either we fall in line and give them our money, or we move toward the Benedict Option, separating ourselves entirely. We either become *like* them or run *from* them. I suggest there's a third option. Let's look to the Word of God, become wise as serpents, and use the enemy's weapons against him.

Special Miracles

A few years ago, God released a radical revelation of abundance into our ministry. At the time, we didn't have a media ministry. I don't even think we had any cameras. When you pastor a small church in the middle of Nowhere, North Carolina, you can easily look at the mega ministries across the country and think, "We could never have that kind of impact." It can be discouraging. However, God spoke to my heart and said these words: *"You don't have to have a mega ministry to have a mega impact."*

As we stood on those words as a congregation, God immediately began to supernaturally supply media equipment. We didn't really know what to do with it, but I began to see a correlation between God's promise and this provision. Media, social media in particular, is a tool that can be used by God to promote any voice He wishes. With today's technology, anyone can post a video that could go viral and reach millions around the world.

What does this all have to do with prayer and spiritual warfare? The pen (media) truly is mightier than the sword. If you and I will become intentional in our use of social media, we can fan the flames of revival around the world. Media can be used as a means to transfer the anointing.

Months before the historic lockdowns of 2020, God visited me in my office while I was praying and said, "I want you to explore what church would look like if it were entirely online." Later on, I understood that this was not an encouragement to shut down the church but rather preparation to supply the needs of thousands who would have no church to go to.

In the fall of 2019, I met with a few of my leaders, and we began to slowly implement strategies that would allow us to really minister to people online. By the time the draconian and unconstitutional shutdowns hit, we were miraculously already in a good position to meet the needs of people around the world. People were not only being saved and discipled, but miracles of healing, deliverance, and provision were taking place online!

And God wrought special miracles by the hands of Paul: so that from his body were brought unto the sick handkerchiefs or aprons, and the diseases departed from them, and the evil spirits went out of them (Acts 19:11-12).

Most of us understand that the tangible power of God can be transferred in unusual ways. It can happen not only through the laying on of hands, but also by the application of a piece of cloth. Demons can be cast out, and diseases can be healed when this anointed fabric connects with the faith of the individual.

The great tent evangelist R.W. Schambach personally told me about one of the most amazing miracles I have ever heard of till this day. He had been known for praying over prayer cloths that would then be taken to the sick and laid on them for healing. Many great miracles happened like this, but one night his faith was challenged.

A woman came to him with a bag of candy. He loved candy, so he took it—thinking it was given to him to eat.

The woman who gave him the candy said, "I want you to wear this candy while you preach under the anointing." At first, he resisted. He didn't want his reputation to be tarnished because he was sending out "prayer candy"!

It sounded foolish, so he recommended that the woman get a prayer cloth and bring that to him instead, but the woman persisted. She explained that her sister had been in a mental hospital for years. She had tried to send her prayer cloths, but the institution had censored her mail. She said, "We're going to put one over on the devil. We're going to cast him out with that candy."[2]

Inspired by her faith, he took the candy, preached with it under the anointing, and gave it back to her. Six months later, two women came down to the altar to place their offerings in the offering bucket at the church where he was preaching. It was the woman who had given him the candy—and her sister! The sister testified that when she bit into the candy, she bit into the power of God. The demon spirits that had oppressed her were cast out, and she came to her right mind and gave her life to Christ!

I'm telling you, God will perform special miracles! The yoke-destroying, burden-removing power of God can be released through cloth or candy, but that's not all. I feel like an announcer on a television show, "But wait—there's more!" If God can heal the sick and set the oppressed free through a cloth, what can He do with a screen? A piece of cloth doesn't speak, but your phone does. If an inanimate object can set the captives free, what can an hour-long video of a powerful sermon do? This is a weapon!

We often wonder in amazement at the miracles in the book of Acts, but I'm here to tell you that we're seeing greater things today already.

> *And when they were come up out of the water, the Spirit of the Lord caught away Philip, that the eunuch saw him no more: and he went on his way rejoicing. But Philip was found at Azotus: and passing through he preached in all the cities, till he came to Caesarea* (Acts 8:39-40).

In one moment, Philip was translated more than twenty-five miles away to preach in a different city. Why? God must have needed him there pronto. How many of us would like to be translated so that the Gospel can be preached? Here's an even more interesting question: would we rather be translated ourselves or have the power to translate anyone we chose? Which is more powerful and effective? Obviously, the ability to translate others.

Do you realize that you have that ability right now? You can go our Encounter Today YouTube channel and by hitting the share button on one of our videos, you can translate me into someone else's home! What would the apostle Paul have thought about such technology? It is truly miraculous, and yet we either yawn at it or ignore it.

Goliath's Sword

Our ministry began to increase in its impact as we focused on our online audience. Let me be clear that we were *not* focused on views, clicks, likes, or shares. We were focused on loving the people. Views and subscribers are vanity metrics that many church leaders will choke on if they're not careful. I've seen it happen. Good ministers can easily get caught up in an unconscious Pavlovian response to these numbers, and they begin to tailor their messages to get more views.

Be forewarned. Don't get hooked on the dopamine rush that's designed by social media companies to suck us into their way of thinking. We must first be sure of what God is telling us to say. Only then can we use the algorithms to our advantage.

As we remained faithful to the message, God began to amplify our voice. All of a sudden, our videos began to reach hundreds of thousands of people. Some, across all platforms, reached more than a million people! In a desperate desire to steward the moment God had given us well, I called out to Him for wisdom. I said, "Lord, what are You doing?" and He said to me, "I'm giving you Goliath's sword, for there is none like it."

> *Then said he unto them, But now, he that hath a purse, let him take it, and likewise his scrip: and he that hath no sword, let him sell his garment, and buy one* (Luke 22:36).

Jesus told His disciples to sell their garments and buy a sword. He told them to monetize and get rid of what they were using to protect themselves from the elements. Why? Because there was a weapon in the enemy's hands that he wanted them to purchase. God is calling every believer to learn how to wield the sword of media.

Don't run from it—redeem it! My son has since learned how to master this weapon and now trains churches how to use it to their advantage. Believers, regardless of age, can learn how to become intentional about liking, commenting on, and sharing the messages their ministry is putting out. This is part of the 21st-century evangelism and prayer.

The enemy wants to use social media to divide and distract us. Let's turn it around and use it to bring us together in prayer and keep the church focused on God's Word. Together, we can dominate the adversary and spread this anointing around the world.

Notes

1. Justin D. Lyons, "On War: Churchill, Thucydides and the Teachable Moment," The Churchill Project: Hillsdale College, January 21, 2019, https://winstonchurchill.hillsdale.edu/thucydides -churchill-parallels.

2. R.W. Schambach, *Miracles* (Shippensburg, PA: Destiny Image Publishers, 2009), 62.

CHAPTER NINE

RISE OF THE SERPENTS

*So shall they fear the name of the Lord from the
west, and his glory from the rising of the sun. When
the enemy shall come in like a flood, the Spirit of the
Lord shall lift up a standard against him.*
—ISAIAH 59:19

"War is the continuation of politics by other means."
—CARL VON CLAUSEWITZ[1]

Now more than ever, it is crucial that the church stand against
the cultural tide. I am not speaking only about the church as an
institution; I am also speaking about the individuals who make
up the church.

It has become increasingly clear that there are fewer ministries and fewer people willing to take that stand at a time when
that stand is vitally important.

On January 20, 2021, Joseph Biden was inaugurated as the 46th president of the United States of America. The consequences that followed were difficult to describe, but the enemy's hand was easy to identify.

It was a time of national division unseen in recent history. Parasitic ideas had infected the American mind, and the church seemed to forget that what was needed was *truth*—and a strong dose of it!

Many fell captive to the enemy at his will as they sided with manipulative politicians who were only interested in their own power. It seemed as though they were trapped in the prison of two ideas and were unable to perceive the wisdom of God.

In the midst of the election chaos, I felt led to look up the word *inauguration*. Webster's defines it as a "ceremonial induction into office."[2] As I read those words, I heard the Lord say, *"I am also performing an inauguration. I am now placing wartime gifts into office, and I am releasing wartime anointings for this new era."*

What's in Your Hand?

Moses was tending his father-in-law Jethro's sheep. As they grazed, he led them through the backside of the desert to the mountain of God, Mount Horeb.

From that spot, God began to speak to Moses through a burning bush. God told Moses that He had seen the bondage of His people, and He wanted Moses to tell Pharaoh to let God's people go.

At this point in history, Pharaoh was the ruler of all Egypt—a kingdom that was vast, mighty, and supremely powerful. It was a kingdom that held the children of Israel in bondage, forcing them to work as slaves.

Moses asked God, "How am I supposed to go against the greatest superpower in the world?"

In turn, God asked Moses, "What's in your hand?"

From this exchange, we can glean insight into another end-time weapon that God is releasing from His arsenal—the staff of Moses (also called the staff of Aaron).

This staff represents the pastoral anointing. In Moses' day, a rod was a simple tool used in the daily operation of guiding the sheep from one grazing location to another. But, when infused with the power of God, Moses' rod became a mighty weapon of deliverance.

In these last days, what was once used for guiding the sheep will be transformed into an end-time weapon. This will show up as radical discipleship that imparts supernatural wisdom and guidance.

Moses was leading natural sheep when God called him to deliver His people, the sheep of His pasture, from the bondage of Egypt. In the same way, God wants to anoint pastors—the shepherds of today—to become a voice of deliverance in the earth. In fact, I believe that the next great wave of deliverance will come through the local church and the pastors who lead them.

We've already learned how important prophetic intelligence is in these last days. God is beginning to raise up pastors who will hear His voice and follow His instructions—those to whom He can download His supernatural wisdom.

The Serpent Is a Weapon

Pharaoh's magicians attempted to display their inaugural powers by mimicking the wonders that Moses performed. When Moses threw down his staff, it turned into a weapon—a divine serpent. Their rods also became serpents—but the divine serpent swallowed them all!

Isn't a serpent a fascinating weapon for God Himself to use? In fact, if you were to look back into the annals of spiritual warfare, you might find this intriguing weapon being used in one of the first spiritual battles in history.

Recorded in Genesis 3:1 is the account of the spiritual battle waged in the Garden of Eden. The first weapon mentioned in this spiritual battle was not a sword, but a serpent:

> *Now the serpent was more subtle than any beast of the field which the Lord God had made* (MEV).

The word *subtle* means shrewd, sensible, cunning. Today, due to the satanic monopoly the enemy has on these characteristics, they tend to have a negative tinge to them, as they should.

However, back when this event took place, it simply meant to exhibit ingenuity or to be artful in planning. This was how God created the serpent.

The snake was not subtle because it was possessed by the devil. It was possessed by the devil *because* it was subtle. The serpent itself became a weapon in the hands of the enemy.

When Aaron threw down his rod, it became a serpent. In certain seasons, that which God uses to pastor and shepherd His people will be used to judge His enemies. At a later time, it will change back into a rod. Being a serpent is not its natural state; it will *assume* this form so it can *consume* all the collective works of the enemy.

When Moses was confronted with this ancient weapon, what did God do? He turned what Moses used for maintenance into a war machine that consumed the enemy's strategic weapons. In this instance, no serpentine weapon of the enemy formed against him could prosper. This wasn't the only time when God took the enemy's weapon and turned it against him.

When the children of Israel rebelled in the wilderness, serpents came and bit them. What did God have Moses do when they were at death's door? God told Moses to construct a serpent and place it on a pole:

> *Then the Lord said to Moses, "Make a fiery serpent, and set it on a pole; and it shall be that everyone who is bitten, when he looks at it, shall live." So Moses made a bronze serpent, and put it on a pole; and so it was, if a serpent had bitten anyone, when he looked at the bronze serpent, he lived* (Numbers 21:8-9 NKJV).

The bronze serpent, fashioned according to the dictates of God, overcame the effects of the serpents that bit the children of Israel. This is essentially the same thing that happened when Moses' rod became a serpent and swallowed up the magician's serpent. The serpent from God overcame the effects of the serpents that came from the enemy—in essence, it became a weapon.

Why? Could it be that victory begins with our willingness to look up and see the spiritual battle that is being waged all around us? In this account, we see the children of Israel looking up to the image of the serpent, and the image of the *harmer* becomes the image of the *healer!* This is similar to the time Moses used a bitter stick to sweeten bitter waters (see Exod. 15:25).

Are you beginning to see God's willingness to use the enemy's weapons against him? Jesus Himself told us to be *"wise as serpents"* (Matt. 10:16). What did Jesus mean? He's not telling them to lurk around in darkness or utter deceitful words. Rather, this is the prudence of winning a war against a seemingly greater foe by using the most effective weapon at hand.

We must be willing to use the best strategies with the best intentions. We have before us the challenge of being both *covert* and *Christian* at the same time.

A Covert Mission that Delivered Israel

When we speak of covert missions in the Bible, the story of Ehud and Eglon comes to mind. The children of Israel were in bondage to their enemy. They were in servitude to the Moabites, and their continual cycle of repentance and deliverance was happening yet again. The story begins in Judges 3:12-15:

> *And the children of Israel again did evil in the sight of the Lord. So the Lord strengthened Eglon*

king of Moab against Israel, because they had done evil in the sight of the Lord. Then he gathered to himself the people of Ammon and Amalek, went and defeated Israel, and took possession of the City of Palms. So the children of Israel served Eglon king of Moab eighteen years.

But when the children of Israel cried out to the Lord, the Lord raised up a deliverer for them: Ehud the son of Gera, the Benjamite, a left-handed man. By him the children of Israel sent tribute to Eglon king of Moab (NKJV).

One of the interesting facts in this account is the description of God's chosen man, Ehud. He was an unlikely deliverer—he was a left-handed man from the tribe of Benjamin, which means "the son of the right hand." Some accounts even indicate that there may have been something wrong with his right hand.

Because of this, it was unlikely he would be looked upon as a threat—in a sense, it allowed Ehud to go on his mission incognito.

On the surface, the mission was simply for Ehud to take the tribute that was due and present it to King Eglon as required. He may have even undertaken this same task many times before. But the real mission was to take out the evil king who held their land captive.

So, this time, Ehud returned to the king's chambers after everyone else had left for home. He told the king that he had a secret message for him from God. The king sent his men away and prepared to listen to the message.

When the message came, it was not the one Eglon expected. The message was Ehud's dagger being thrust into the king's belly—a belly so fat the dagger disappeared, remaining inside the king and taking his life. Neither the king nor his cohorts suspected Ehud of being capable of such an act—killing the king in cold blood. But because of this act, Israel was able to rally and conquer the Moabites, gaining their freedom once again.

While you may not be called upon to kill a king (this is a different era), you have been called to triumph over the enemy using the wisdom of God.

> *I wisdom dwell with prudence, and find out knowledge of witty inventions* (Proverbs 8:12).

I believe God is raising up some Ehuds that will come against the Eglons of our day. He will cause you to become "wise as a serpent," even becoming crafty and covert in the spirit, well able to do what He has called you to do. When that time comes, God will surely place His spiritual weapon of choice into your hand, and He will instruct you how to use it.

Are You a Donkey or a Viper?

Being concerned about the current political scene is not something new. In 1712, Reverend Thomas Bradbury preached a message entitled "The Ass or the Serpent, A Comparison Between the Tribes of Issachar and Dan, in their Regard for Civil Liberty." It was later republished in Massachusetts in 1744 as a prophetic word for the time leading up to the revolution. It is believed that it was this sermon that inspired the "Don't Tread on Me" Flag.

Being inspired by Bradbury's comparison between these two sons of Jacob, I took a deeper look into the social and spiritual implications of the traits of Dan and Issachar.

As Jacob was dying, he described the natures of his twelve sons, and my, how different they were. It was a reminder that "all are not Israel who are of Israel" (see Rom. 9:6). The Spirit of God came upon Jacob, and he prophesied concerning their futures.

He called all twelve of his sons together—each son being the head of entire tribe. Imagine the family reunion that took place that day! Genesis 49:1-2 records:

> *And Jacob called his sons and said, "Gather together, that I may tell you what shall befall you in the last days: Gather together and hear, you sons of Jacob, and listen to Israel your father"* (NKJV).

Jacob began by addressing Reuben, the firstborn, and then continued speaking in turn to each son. Verses 14-18 record the prophecies to Dan and Issachar:

> *Issachar is a strong donkey, lying down between two burdens; he saw that rest was good, and that the land was pleasant; he bowed his shoulder to bear a burden, and became a band of slaves.*
>
> *Dan shall judge his people as one of the tribes of Israel. Dan shall be a serpent by the way, a viper by the path, that bites the horse's heels, so that its rider shall fall backward. I have waited for your salvation, O Lord!* (NKJV)

Following these prophecies, Jacob gave his family instructions regarding his burial, and then *"breathed his last, and was gathered to his people"* (Gen. 49:33).

Jacob condemned the passive obedience of Issachar. He compared him to one of the most stubborn animals in creation, the donkey, lamenting how the tribe of Issachar would bow to the tyranny of an oppressor and fall into servitude.

Issachar and his brethren were a strong tribe, but they stubbornly refused to use that strength. Renouncing the warlike spirit of the children of Israel, they preferred instead to labor in the luxurious repose of fat pastures. Too self-satisfied to fight for their freedom, they resigned themselves to the task of laboring for the benefit of others at the expense of their own future. They settled into a life of agriculture and oppression—growing crops for others—instead of a life of military prowess and advancement. This tribe certainly had positive characteristics that we should emulate, but we must also learn from their failures.

In the modern church of today, this would translate into a church whose primary goal was to grow by accumulating people. After all, the church growth gurus tell us that *people in the pews equates to dollars in the plates.*

A church with an Issachar spirit is not one willing to take on the culture war necessary to produce change in society. Instead, this is a church willing to forsake its God-given potential for the transient blessing of prosperity—all is good if we are making money or are taken care of.

An Issachar spirit is one that is more focused on entertainment than exertion—they *"saw that rest was good."* This was a people content to go to work, come home, watch a movie, and do it all again the next day. This was a people to whom rest and recreation were more valuable than freedom.

Dan, on the other hand, judged his people and led by example. He was a leader who governed well, and his people enjoyed independence as a result. He was not one to give in when the enemy advanced against him. This stubbornness may later get Dan into trouble but, when tempered, it was something to be admired.

Like a serpent in the road, the tribe of Dan would strike back when trampled underfoot. They would not allow oppression to gain a foothold. Like a viper biting the hoof of a horse on the path, the tribe of Dan would confront tyranny and injustice, using what their enemy meant for evil and turning it to their good.

God describes the wisdom of this tribe by calling them serpents. They were willing to put themselves in harm's way. They would rather risk being crushed by the hooves of a horse than to slither off and stagnate on the sidelines and lose their inheritance.

Being a serpent would give them an edge in attaining victory. If they couldn't overthrow the tyrants by blunt force, they would bite their horses' heels so that the riders would be overthrown. They would endeavor to bring down a tyrant by his own methods if all the rest should fail. If they could not stop him by other means, they would have his own horse throw him.

The mindset of the tribe of Dan represents that of a church not willing to remain in bondage to the culture of the day. This is a church who will break free from the cult of entertainment. Life for them is more than living vicariously through the lives of others portrayed on the silver screen.

Life for them is standing up against the societal norms and carving out their own path. This is a church that will reach out into the highways and byways and establish a beachhead of freedom, not just for themselves but for their whole tribe. This is a tribe who will take responsibility for their own future and not depend on someone else to procure it for them.

The choice looming before both the church and the churchgoers is clear: will you be like Issachar and depend on others to take care of you, or will you be like Dan and take responsibility for yourself?

Politicians and preachers alike have taken advantage of this disparity of mindset. Diving down the rabbit hole of conspiracy theories, many Christians were—and still are—waiting on some unseen force or unnamed operative to save the day.

This was not the blessing intended for the children of Israel, nor is it the blessing intended for the church today. God is looking for a prophetic people who will recognize that God is going to equip *them* to become the answer to the issues of the day.

When we are under attack is not the time to sit back and wait for someone to come to our aid. Rather, it is the time to become proactive and take action ourselves.

If there's one thing we've learned, it is that if you want something done right, you've got to do it yourself. Now is the time for civic education and involvement. We can no longer sit idly by and wait for someone else to do the work God has called us to do.

How many times have you depended on an "expert" to take care of an issue for you, and their efforts have turned out to be incomplete, unnecessarily expensive, or just plain wrong?

What I want you to realize is that when you are operating in the wisdom of God, you are the expert! You are the one God has called to become part of a radical remnant. You are the one who represents the rise of the serpents—God's end-time militia, not complacent and compliant like Issachar, but proactive and preemptive like Dan.

The sons of Issachar are often hailed for their ability to discern the times and the seasons (see 1 Chron. 12:32). This is an important characteristic, and we certainly need more of this in the church today. However, if you have no backbone, when you discern a wrong environment, you will find yourself *conforming* to it instead of *confronting* it. We need Issachar's discernment to converge with Dan's boldness.

A donkey doesn't pose much of a threat to anyone, except perhaps when it exerts its stubborn streak and won't help you get your work done! A viper is dangerous because of what is in its mouth. Satan is terrified of the power your words have. Bold, loving, and faith-filled words are weapons against the enemy's agenda.

The Word of Faith Renewal

If we wish to be armed for victory, we must sharpen this weapon. The Word of Faith renewal came to the body of Christ for this purpose. God has spent decades attempting to train the church to sharpen their confession. This was a vital step in the church's journey to victory, but many today want to divorce themselves from the truths revived in this movement.

You might have had a bad experience with someone claiming to be "Word of Faith." What does that have to do with the eternal truth of the power of your words? We will not move forward in this next great awakening unless we honor and guard the truths that God has revived in the last century. Our words matter!

The children of Israel were not able to possess the land because they allowed the weapon of confession to become dull—and harmful only to themselves. They wanted to accomplish through force what could only be accomplished through the Word of God.

If thou hast done foolishly in lifting up thyself, or if thou hast thought evil, lay thine hand upon thy mouth (Proverbs 30:32).

Part of the process of sharpening this weapon of speaking faith-filled words is learning to be quiet. This verse is telling us to put armed guards around our mouths. In war, it's always important to guard your weapons—and your mouth is an armory full of weapons!

Those who have experience handling weapons are terrified when they see someone pick up a gun, put their finger on the trigger, and point it in their direction. I don't care what your intentions are—take your finger off the trigger and point that weapon somewhere else! Anyone who doesn't take the gun seriously is a danger to themselves and those around them. The same is true when it comes to the confession of our mouths.

We don't play around with guns when they are loaded. We should *always* assume they are loaded. In the same way, we should regard our mouths as "loaded." We need to be disciplined with our words because they are powerful:

A man's belly shall be satisfied with the fruit of his mouth; and with the increase of his lips shall he be filled. Death and life are in the power of the tongue: and they that love it shall eat the fruit thereof (Proverbs 18:20-21).

When Jesus called the Pharisees a generation of vipers (see Matt. 12:34), He was referring to how dangerous everything they said was. Again, a viper's danger comes from its mouth— it poisons everything it puts its mouth on. What have you poisoned with words that were not of God? How many relationships have been destroyed or prayers hindered by people who don't take their words seriously enough?

O generation of vipers, how can ye, being evil, speak good things? for out of the abundance of the heart the mouth speaketh. A good man out of the good treasure of the heart bringeth forth good things: and an evil man out of the evil treasure bringeth forth evil things. But I say unto you, That every idle word that men shall speak, they shall give account thereof in the day of judgment. For by thy words thou shalt be justified, and by thy words thou shalt be condemned (Matthew 12:34-37).

God considers this weapon so powerful that He is keeping a log and warning us that we will give an account for every idle word we speak. He doesn't just warn us against cursing or speaking evil words, but He also threatens us with punishment for every idle word. An idle word is a word not meant to go anywhere. Think of your car when it's idling—it's running, but it's not going anywhere. Many times, we're just running our mouths, but we're not accomplishing anything with them. These are idle words:

> *There is that speaketh like the piercings of a sword: but the tongue of the wise is health* (Proverbs 12:18).

When we repeat what the enemy says, those words are like sharp swords that pierce the heart. But when we say what God says, our words can bring healing.

I learned this lesson firsthand through an experience I had. I recount this story in my book *The Ephesian Mandate*. I have included it here to show you how God impressed upon me the power of the spoken Word:

> I remember one time we had a house with a glass door, with one step down into the yard. At the time, a pack of stray dogs kept running through our yard. I kept a BB gun ready so that anytime I saw them, I could run outside and shoot toward them—not to hurt them, but to scare them away.

> One particular day, I saw them converging on my back yard. I grabbed the BB gun and headed toward

the door. I was so totally focused on dealing with the stray dogs that I didn't see the aquarium sitting on the step just outside the door. It was below my line of sight, and mostly transparent, because it was also made of glass.

In my haste to get outside, I pushed the door open, and it hit the aquarium. The door stopped, but I didn't. My momentum propelled me right through that glass door, down the step and through the air about five feet out into the yard. I felt like I was in a scene from an action movie—shattered glass from the door was flying all around me, the door was banging, and I'm shouting. My wife yells from the other room, "Are you okay?"

You know what goes through your mind? You can get upset with somebody very quickly, and have good justification for it. She had to have heard what sounded like the house falling down, and she's not even coming to see! One of my children is playing a video game nearby and barely even notices....

"Are you okay?" Really? Am I okay? My first reaction was to begin to yell, "NO! What do you think? I fell through a glass door, flew five feet through the air. I'm probably cut up, and probably broke some bones..." Let me tell you, I am sprawled on the ground in the midst of all of that shattered glass, and the moment I let the word "No!" come out of my mouth, the Holy Ghost apprehended me and said, "What's the matter with you?"

Well, my first reaction, of course, from years of train-ing was to think, "Of course I'm not okay. How could I be?" All our lives we have been schooled in doubt and unbelief, so our first reaction is to speak that doubt and unbelief. Once we have been exposed to the Word of God, the Holy Ghost will not let us get away with that. As an active agent in Creation, He fully understands the power of the spoken Word.

And laying there, before I could even check to see if I was cut, bleeding, or otherwise injured, I had to say, "Lord I repent. I repent right now. In the name of Jesus, I am okay!" And guess what? I didn't have a scratch; I didn't have a bruise. The only thing injured was my pride. Everything else was fine.[3]

In that moment, I had a choice. I could either act on my own natural knowledge—slamming through a glass door will result in bodily injury—or the truth that God was revealing to me: *"the word is nigh thee, even in thy mouth, and in thy heart: that is, the word of faith"* (Rom. 10:8). I am thankful I chose to repent and speak the Word. Injured pride is far easier to deal with than an injured body!

The power of the Word of God is activated when it is revealed to you and released when you speak it. When you speak it, it becomes a *rhema* word—a revealed word that is a right now word for your situation.

When Jesus came into the coasts of Caesarea Philippi, he asked his disciples, saying, Whom do men say that I the Son of man am? And they said, Some say that thou art John the Baptist: some, Elias; and others, Jeremias, or one of the prophets. He saith unto them, But whom say ye that I am? And Simon Peter answered and said, Thou art the Christ, the Son of the living God. And Jesus answered and said unto him, Blessed art thou, Simon Barjona: for flesh and blood hath not revealed it unto thee, but my Father which is in heaven (Matthew 16:13-17).

He had a *rhema* word. A *rhema* word is a weaponized word for the Kingdom.

And I say also unto thee, That thou art Peter, and upon this rock I will build my church; and the gates of hell shall not prevail against it. And I will give unto thee the keys of the kingdom of heaven: and whatsoever thou shalt bind on earth shall be bound in heaven: and whatsoever thou shalt loose on earth shall be loosed in heaven (Matthew 16:18-19).

When a revealed word is spoken, it becomes a weapon. Jesus gave Peter a sword; He has given us a sword, too. Sharpen your sword by only saying what He says, and you'll be armed for victory.

Notes

1. "What Is War?" in Carl von Clausewitz, Col. J.J. Graham, trans., *On War, New and Revised edition with Introduction and Notes by Col. F.N. Maude, in Three Volumes*, Vol. 1 (London: Kegan Paul, Trench, Trubner & C., 1918).

2. *Merriam-Webster's Online Dictionary*, s.v. "Inauguration," accessed December 5, 2021, https://www.merriam-webster.com/dictionary/inauguration.

3. Alan Didio, *The Ephesian Mandate*, 81.

CHAPTER TEN

THE VISION OF APOLLYON

And they had a king over them, which is the angel of the bottomless pit, whose name in the Hebrew tongue is Abaddon, but in the Greek tongue hath his name Apollyon.

—REVELATION 9:11

"It was one of those pictures which are so contrived that the eyes follow you about when you move. *Big Brother Is Watching You*, the caption beneath it ran."

—GEORGE ORWELL, *1984*[1]

Sleep was never a priority for him, but on this night, Dr. Lester Sumrall could find little rest. Close to midnight, when he had been sleeping only a short while, he was suddenly awakened.

He had received a startling dream from the Lord. He dreamed that just above him was a huge television. Two eyes were glaring back at him through the screen, and a voice said, "I am not a scarecrow. I am Apollyon!"[2]

Dr. Sumrall had been writing a book for almost two years called *Scarecrow*. He had attempted to finish it many times, but without success. The main premise of the book was that the devil was nothing more than a scarecrow, a *"flap in the breeze."* As he trembled in his bed, the mere thought of this book left him ashamed.

Later, when he would teach on this dream, Dr. Sumrall would liken the eyes on the screen to "Big Brother" from George Orwell's classic novel *1984*. We will revisit this prophetic comparison in a moment.

When he asked the Lord what this dream meant, he said the Spirit of God told him that commercial television would damn this nation and damn the world—and that television had released three evil spirits upon the world:

1. A mocking spirit against God

2. Demonic music

3. A spirit of the occult

It is startling that long before the smartphone, the proliferation of the internet, or social media, this prophetic voice would see a Big Brother-like demonic force that would destroy America and the world through a screen. We are seeing its fulfillment in our time, and we must rise to the occasion. There is a demonic and humanistic showdown that's taking place right now. The nations of the world are on a razor's edge.

An Orwellian Prophecy

The Greek word *Apollyon* means "destroyer." If the eyes are the windows to the soul, we can learn a lot about our enemy by looking directly into his eyes (see Matt. 6:22-23). Dr. Sumrall looked into the eyes of the destroyer and saw an Orwellian figure. If we can understand our enemy's devices, we can get the advantage and win the war (see 2 Cor. 2:11). Let's take a look and see where those eyes were first prophesied.

On an island in the Hebrides off the coast of Scotland, grieving the death of his wife, a famous author began to write. The novel *1984*, which was written only months before his own death, is George Orwell's story of a world gripped by the evils of totalitarianism. The story tells of events after a global war in which the nations of the world coalesce to end violence through tyranny.

It immediately became a best seller. George Orwell, whose given name was Eric Blair, laid out a stunning picture of what a fear-driven society would look like. Even today, we can see the same seeds of tyranny in the policies advocated by those who demand their version of tolerance. Some have rightly questioned whether *1984* was a novel or a prophecy.

In amazing detail, he describes a government that polices thought. Menacing signs and screens are everywhere with the chilling words, "*Big Brother Is Watching You.*"

In this far-fetched society, the media was called "The Ministry of Truth." They also called the war department "The Ministry of Peace," showing how they manipulated the meaning of words as part of their strategy of control. Even science and math had become politicized as they manipulated the citizens to believe that 2+2=5.

Why was it so important to get the citizens to believe that 2+2=5? It was the gateway to control—if you can get someone to say something is *true* that they know to be *false*, you can get them to do anything.

We see the same thing happening today when the state-run media uses phrases like "pro-choice" or "love wins." New laws are being implemented around the world that would make it illegal to say that a man is not a woman and a woman is not a man. Even biology is becoming politicized.

Society itself is compelling us to say things we know to be false in the name of inclusion or tolerance. As people of "The Way, The Truth, and The Life," we must never allow falsities to come out of our mouths (see John 14:6). We speak the truth in love (see Eph. 4:15).

The eerie part of Orwell's story is that he described a time when there were screens in every home. These screens were installed to give the government the ability to see and hear everything that went on in people's private lives. The Thought Police invaded every home and every street corner.

Orwell described a time when the government would be able to speak to everyone in the whole nation at once through these screens. Long before all the modern tech advances of our time, he was predicting the complete subjugation of the human person through the screen.

I believe that this is what Dr. Lester Sumrall saw. He saw the eyes of "Big Brother" influencing the nation through the very screen you probably have within your reach right now. If it weren't for the revivals of the twentieth century, we would already be there. The healing movement, the Word of Faith renewal, the prosperity movement, the charismatic renewal, and the moral majority have all helped to slow the advance of this destructive spirit.

However, in recent years we have come to a tipping point. Politicians and media moguls have mastered these Orwellian tactics of division. We can see it everywhere. Pitting us one against the other, they've managed to control us. Without agreement, we lose our power in prayer. The spirit of the age is working to divide us and to contaminate our agreement.

> *Again I say unto you, That if two of you shall agree on earth as touching any thing that they shall ask, it shall be done for them of my Father which is in heaven* (Matthew 18:19).

Politics and Polarization

At the end of World War II, a known occultist and friend of Franklin Delano Roosevelt, Manly P. Hall, told the president that this world was broken and needed to be fixed. In the spring of 1944, he said:

> To make things right we will have to undo much that is cherished error. The [current] problem of revising the Bible shows how difficult it is to do this. For the last hundred years we have been trying to get out an edition of the Bible that is reasonably correct, but nobody wants it. What's wanted is the good old King James Version, every jot and tittle of it![3]

Who was this occultist working with to create a new translation of the Bible—and why? Were they ever successful, and is that translation in circulation today? These are questions for another day, but I want to you see how this destructive spirit has been working its way into the nation and the church.

In that edition of his magazine, he went on say that over the next 10 years they would need to rebuild society. Their goals would be a world police force, a world council, and a world religion. What could hinder their grand plan? The kind of people who cling to their Bibles!

The biggest threat to the spirit of this age is a Bible-believing church and a Bible-believing Christian. This spirit doesn't care if you attend church or get slain in the Spirit, as long as you don't hold on to, read, and believe your Bible.

In order to get people to let go of this "cherished error" and embrace Hall's idea of a new world order, they would need to condition the public. The way of conditioning would be the one used in Central Europe to condition Nazi minds. There, the circulation of an ideology began in the public schools. He told them they had to begin with small children, and that it would take five generations.

In the 1940s, this influential occultist, who had significant influence in the White House, declared that they would need at least five generations before they could create a world capable of receiving these ideas. Count them down:

1. Baby Boomers
2. Gen X

3. Millennials

4. Gen Z

We are now entering the fifth generation. We are one generation away from *1984*. Those old-timers who used to cling to their Bible (every jot and tittle) are dying out. We have new leadership gurus who tell us that if we want to remain relevant, we must detach ourselves from the Word of God. Even in Spirit-filled communities, we have too many people having "out-of-Bible experiences."

According to people like Mr. Hall, the only thing hindering progress is those people who believe in an old-fashioned and outdated Gospel. I want to go on record right now and say that I still believe *The Book!* Every jot and tittle! It's time to get back to the sure foundation of the Word of God—and it starts with you. Make Bible reading a priority in your house, and don't support ministries who fail to do the same.

In an effort to cut off the church's potential impact on society, the world has managed to compartmentalize us by politicizing us (as if the Body of Christ could fit into one party or the other), and we bought into it—hook, line, and sinker. I want to reiterate what I stated earlier: it's not that the church shouldn't be involved in politics, but politics should not be involved in the church. We've traded our prophetic anointing for a partisan one. When this happens, the political debate becomes a sinking ship.

It's a trap! The spirit of anti-Christ is a divisive spirit, and it will blind the minds of those who cater to it.

Are we supposed to be involved in politics? Yes, but we must not lose our prophetic edge and allow ourselves to be manipulated and marginalized by this demonic spirit. Until we learn this, all our political debates won't amount to a pile of ash when compared to the eternal good that could have come from spending that time and effort being salt and light, teaching men and women to hear the voice of God. If everyone who criticized our political leaders prayed for them with soul-hot intercession, we'd have a nationwide revival within a week.

Dr. Lester Sumrall saw all of this in his dream. The polarization that's happening in this nation and the church is coming through that screen. How can we fight back?

Here is the crux of the issue:

> *For we wrestle not against flesh and blood, but against principalities, against powers, against the rulers of the darkness of this world, against spiritual wickedness in high places* (Ephesians 6:12).

Apollyon is a spiritual enemy arrayed against the church. Big Brother—and by that I am referring to the current political climate, the potential Orwellian police state, social media, or any other form of cultural control—is a natural enemy.

Big Brother seeks to control us from the outside in, through unconstitutional legislation, economic control, and power grabs. Apollyon seeks to control us from the inside out. Apollyon wants us to trade what we believe for what they want us to believe.

We can, to some extent, come against the constraints in the natural and gain some success. We can't, however, wage war against a spiritual enemy through natural means.

In these perilous times, then, where can we go to find help? Where can we go to find the weapons that we need to win this fight? God's house is the only place from which the army of God can mount a reasonable offense. The problem is that while we were distracted by the media, we abandoned God's house. As we return, we find it has fallen into disrepair.

A Return to the House of the Lord

If we want to be fully equipped and armed for victory, we must rediscover a passion for the house of God:

> *In the second year of Darius the king, in the sixth month, in the first day of the month, came the word of the Lord by Haggai the prophet unto Zerubbabel the son of Shealtiel, governor of Judah, and to Joshua the son of Josedech, the high priest, saying, Thus speaketh the Lord of hosts, saying, This people say, The time is not come, the time that the Lord's house should be built. Then came the word of the Lord by Haggai the prophet, saying, Is it time for you, O ye, to dwell in your cieled houses, and this house lie waste? Now therefore thus saith the Lord of hosts; Consider your ways. Ye have sown much, and bring in little; ye eat, but ye have not enough; ye drink, but ye are not filled with drink; ye clothe you, but there is none warm; and he that earneth*

wages earneth wages to put it into a bag with holes.
Thus saith the Lord of hosts; Consider your ways.
Go up to the mountain, and bring wood, and build
the house; and I will take pleasure in it, and I will
be glorified, saith the Lord. Ye looked for much,
and, lo, it came to little; and when ye brought it
home, I did blow upon it. Why? saith the Lord of
hosts. Because of mine house that is waste, and ye
run every man unto his own house. Therefore the
heaven over you is stayed from dew, and the earth is
stayed from her fruit (Haggai 1:1-10).

There were three minor prophets who were the last to speak chronologically in the Old Covenant: Haggai, Zechariah, and Malachi. After this, there were 400 years of silence until John the Baptist. They are called minor prophets because of the short time they ministered to the nation of Israel. Prophets like Isaiah and Jeremiah ministered for over 40 years, whereas Haggai's work only spanned a few months.

These minor prophets are called "post-exilic prophets" because they came on the scene after the exile. They were part of the "coming home again"—a new beginning, a restoration.

The Persian king, Cyrus, who had conquered Babylon, had agreed to allow the captive Jews to return to their homeland and rebuild the house of God—if they would promise to pray for him. Though he liberated them and gave them permission to return home, only 50,000 did so.

Why would anyone choose to remain with their captors? By this time, most of them had been born into exile. They didn't know anything else. Many of them had jobs in Babylon and were quite comfortable.

Those who did return were led by two men. One was a prince named Zerubbabel. He had been born in exile, but he was the only surviving member of the royal line of David. The second was a priest coincidentally named Joshua. These men, and those who returned with them, were not motivated by comfort or economics. The land hadn't been cultivated in seventy years. There was going to be a difficult road ahead for them—and they knew it.

They were going back to a city whose walls had been broken down. They were going back to a city where they would be surrounded by people who had compromised their faith and didn't want them around. These people were the Samaritans. In fact, the Samaritans had such a bad reputation that Jesus offended the crowd when he spoke of a "good" Samaritan (see Luke 10:25-37).

These were major challenges, but those who did return weren't motivated by greed or personal comfort. They were motivated by one driving vision—rebuild the house of God.

Paying the Price but Missing the Point

All this was a great sacrifice. They left their families, their friends, and the security of their jobs. They left their brick-built homes for tents, and they left prosperity for uncertainty. They left trading for agriculture. They were going to have to learn how to dig again.

They were willing to endure all this if it meant that the glory of God would return to His people. They said, "If this is the price of seeing the glory, I'll gladly pay it."

It is a question we have to ask ourselves. Are we willing to leave the place of comfort we've spent years developing if it means that God will be glorified? Are we willing to wade back out into the waters of uncertainty? Now, you can see why so few returned to Jerusalem.

There were so few of them that they had to start by building a small temple. They were happy to start with what they had until the dream gave way to reality. The size of their task and the opposition of the locals wearied them. Even the financial assistance that Cyrus had promised to fund their rebuilding was cut off when Darius came into power. After only two years of construction, they stopped building.

For the next sixteen years, they didn't do anything to build or improve the house of God. All they had were the foundations and some low walls. They comforted themselves with a familiar trope: "God understands." After all, they were struggling to stay alive and feed their families. Certainly, God would understand if the construction of His house were to take a back seat for a little while!

Then a recession hit. Bad harvests, droughts, and disease. One bad event piled on top of another, and they began to cry out to God, "Why have You allowed this to happen? We left everything to follow and honor You!"

Excuses started rolling in to make sense of the seemingly false prophecies of hope and glory. "Maybe it was the wrong time. Maybe we should have saved more. Maybe we jumped out in faith too soon." It had been eighteen years since they returned. This was when Haggai began to prophesy.

As you read the book of Haggai, you get the sense that God is tired of the excuses. They had been saying that they couldn't focus on His house because of their own problems, but the truth was that all their problems stemmed from them *not* focusing on His house.

Their priorities had gotten turned upside down, and they couldn't see it. Their most effective weapon against their current problems was to rebuild the house of God. But they were missing the point altogether. I will tell you what they were missing in a moment.

God began to interrogate His people through Haggai by asking tough questions. The problem with that was that people in general don't like to think deeply or honestly about things. We prefer bumper sticker slogans and answers that feed our emotions and allow us to remain irresponsible. The people had begun to think that God was doing this to them, but Haggai showed them that as soon as they stopped putting God's house first, everything fell apart. They were doing it to themselves.

Miraculously, the people received his message and began to build once again. But just one month later, morale began to erode again. People started to gossip and complain about the work they were doing. "You call this a temple?" How many people today fail to finish what God has called them to do because they don't think it's good enough? The enemy loves to manipulate perfectionists. But in this case, the enemy was correct—what they were doing wasn't good enough because they were still missing the point. *They were still addressing a spiritual problem through natural means.*

They pressed on, knowing that a small house for God was better than no house—but the drought was relentless. After two months, the people started to turn on Haggai. They were questioning why God had not sent any rain. "Were the prophecies wrong?" The answer was simple. They were trying to build a holy thing with unholy hands:

> *Thus saith the Lord of hosts; Ask now the priests concerning the law, saying, If one bear holy flesh in the skirt of his garment, and with his skirt do touch bread, or pottage, or wine, or oil, or any meat, shall it be holy? And the priests answered and said, No. Then said Haggai, If one that is unclean by a dead body touch any of these, shall it be unclean? And the priests answered and said, It shall be unclean. Then answered Haggai, and said, So is this people, and so is this nation before me, saith the Lord; and so is every work of their hands; and that which they offer there is unclean* (Haggai 2:11-14).

According to the historical record, they once again heeded the word, repented, and the rain began to fall the next day!

What is God trying to say to us prophetically? Seek first His Kingdom and all these things will be added to you (see Matt. 6:33). We get so busy with our daily responsibilities that we often forget to put God's house first. God's house is a weapon against the forces of darkness, and we often yield this ground, thinking, "God understands." We need to be serving, giving, and praying in the house of God if we want the windows of Heaven to be opened for us.

The Wind from the Treasury

There is about to be an unparalleled manifestation of God's glory in His house. *This is what they were missing, and we will miss it as well if we can't see beyond our service "in the temple."* If we are looking at natural means to solve spiritual problems, we will miss it every time.

The purpose of the temple was not to provide the king with a place where his subjects could pray for him, as noble as that sounds. The purpose of the temple was, and had always been, and will always be, the place where God has chosen to meet with His people.

The captives who had returned to Jerusalem were not able to stay with the rebuilding program because they kept losing heart. They were struggling to accomplish a spiritual task through natural means. Although natural means can have good effects, they are not the complete solution:

> *For bodily exercise profiteth little: but godliness is profitable unto all things, having promise of the life that now is, and of that which is to come* (1 Timothy 4:8).

What they needed was not an increased budget or better building materials; what they needed was an infusion of the power that could only come from an encounter with God Himself in the Holy Place.

It is what the church needs today. We need to encounter the life-changing and life-sustaining power of God on a personal level. *The only way we will ever be able to change the culture is by being changed ourselves!*

The soldiers in Hezekiah's day went to the House in the Forest to find the weaponry they needed. We can do the same. We can return to the house of the Lord.

Rebuilding the house of God is more than serving, ushering, working in the nursery, or singing in the choir. Rebuilding the house of God is more than showing up on a workday, painting a classroom, or teaching a Sunday school class.

Rebuilding the house of God is finding that place of communion with God. It is about connecting with that place within your spirit where God dwells. It is about being alone until you aren't alone anymore. It is about experiencing the wind of God breathing life into you in the secret place:

> *The Lord makes the clouds rise from far across the earth, and he makes lightning to go with the rain. Then from his secret place he sends out the wind* (Psalm 135:7 CEV).

The King James Version of this verse says, "*he bringeth the wind out of his treasuries.*" Throughout Scripture, wind is analogous to the Holy Spirit, the *ruach* of God. It is only when we have been empowered by the Holy Spirit that we will have the ability to influence our surroundings. A person who has been empowered by the Holy Spirit is the ultimate culture influencer!

The wind, the *ruach* of God, the Holy Spirit, is the highest and best weapon in the arsenal of God. Here is how it began:

> *And when the day of Pentecost was fully come, they were all with one accord in one place. And suddenly*

there came a sound from heaven as of a rushing mighty wind, and it filled all the house where they were sitting. And there appeared unto them cloven tongues like as of fire, and it sat upon each of them. And they were all filled with the Holy Ghost, and began to speak with other tongues, as the Spirit gave them utterance (Acts 2:1-4).

The wind of God, the Holy Spirit, blew into the Upper Room and transformed the disciples from the inside out. From that moment, they were empowered to take on their culture and make a difference everywhere they went. This transformation, the Baptism of the Holy Spirit, is available to every believer. All we have to do is ask:

If ye then, being evil, know how to give good gifts unto your children: how much more shall your heavenly Father give the Holy Spirit to them that ask him? (Luke 11:13)

The Bible calls the Holy Spirit the *Paraclete*, the one called alongside to help us. Jesus said that He would send the Holy Spirit to live on the inside of us and to be with us forever:

And I will pray the Father, and he shall give you another Comforter, that he may abide with you for ever; even the Spirit of truth; whom the world cannot receive, because it seeth him not, neither knoweth him: but ye know him; for he dwelleth with you, and shall be in you (John 14:16-17).

This weapon from the armory of God will empower us to face down Apollyon in our lives and to confront the evils of our day—not in our own strength, but in the power of the Holy Spirit. The Bible prophesies that we will wield a weapon of great strength and power—out of our bellies will flow rivers of living waters.

> *In the last day, that great day of the feast, Jesus stood and cried, saying, If any man thirst, let him come unto me, and drink. He that believeth on me, as the scripture hath said, out of his belly shall flow rivers of living water. (But this spake he of the Spirit, which they that believe on him should receive: for the Holy Ghost was not yet given; because that Jesus was not yet glorified)* (John 7:37-39).

The power of a river is undisputed. Across this great country are numerous power plants situated on rivers where they operate by the power of the flowing water (run-of-the-river hydroelectricity).

The flowing river represents the Holy Spirit. When we allow Him to flow through us in prayer, we are generating supernatural energy that will cause us to become His witnesses—in Jerusalem, Judea, Samaria, and the uttermost part of the earth.

> *And, being assembled together with them, commanded them that they should not depart from Jerusalem, but wait for the promise of the Father, which, saith he, ye have heard of me. For John truly baptized with water; but ye shall be baptized with the Holy Ghost not many days hence.*

...But ye shall receive power, after that the Holy Ghost is come upon you: and ye shall be witnesses unto me both in Jerusalem, and in all Judaea, and in Samaria, and unto the uttermost part of the earth (Acts 1:4-5, 8).

I encourage you to find a place of prayer, ask God to fill you with the Holy Spirit, and expect all your Jerusalems, Judeas, Samarias, and uttermost parts of your life to be touched. When you pray, rivers of living water will flow out of your belly, or spirit. Like the disciples on the Day of Pentecost, you too, can pray in the Spirit:

Likewise the Spirit also helpeth our infirmities: for we know not what we should pray for as we ought: but the Spirit itself maketh intercession for us with groanings which cannot be uttered. And he that searcheth the hearts knoweth what is the mind of the Spirit, because he maketh intercession for the saints according to the will of God (Romans 8:26-27).

With this endowment of power, you will become more effective in prayer than you have ever been. You may not know exactly how to pray for the situations that come before you, but the Holy Spirit does. You will be armed for victory by the greatest prayer strategist of all, the Holy Spirit Himself!

Notes

1. George Orwell, *1984* (New York: Signet Classics, 1950).

2. David Krienke, "Dr. Lester Sumrall's Apollyon Dream," YouTube, December 17, 2019, https:/www .youtube.com/watch?v=__DP9H7UbN8.

3. Johnny Cirucci, "Vatican Freemasons Control All Reality From 'Science' To 'Shakespeare,'" May 14, 2021, https://johnnycirucci.com/vatican -freemasons-control-all-reality.

CHAPTER ELEVEN

OPERATION UNDERWORLD

How wonderful, how beautiful, when brothers and sisters get along! It's like costly anointing oil.
—PSALM 133:1-2, MSG

"Fredo, you're my older brother, and I love you. But don't ever take sides with anyone against the family again. Ever."
—MICHAEL CORLEONE, *The Godfather*

After the attack on Pearl Harbor, the United States was still scrambling to engage in a war for which it was frightfully unprepared. German naval submarines, called U-boats, were stalking the coasts of America. It had been reported that not only did Hitler have submarines operating off American shores, he had also had spies infiltrating key positions in American industry.

This turned out to be alarmingly true. Hitler not only wanted to know every American secret, but he also wanted to have his spies conduct terrorist attacks by starting strategic industrial fires. One suspected attack was the fire that destroyed the USS Lafayette in New York City.

In addition, the Allies were about to conduct one of the boldest moves in military history: the allied invasion of Sicily. This little island off the coast of Italy was a key strategic position that the Allies needed in order to take back Nazi-occupied Europe, but they couldn't get locals to work with them.

An Unlikely Alliance

In times of war, you need unlikely allies. The Manhattan district attorney's office as well as the U.S. Military saw an interesting common denominator with these two problems.

The Allies needed Sicilian cooperation to conduct the invasion of Sicily, and the city of New York needed eyes on the docks to spot spies or potential U-boat activity.

Between the world wars, masses of Italian immigrants had flooded into America. Many came through Ellis Island and took up residence in New York. As it is with any massive influx of people, the people's culture came with the people. With this population, that meant the mafia.

The mafia's power and influence grew during this time, and though United States law enforcement officials weren't saying much publicly, there was a war going on to root out this corruption and shut the mafia down. However, now the Sicilian mafia were the only ones who had controlling interests on both fronts—New York City and the island of Sicily.

Enter Charles "Lucky" Luciano, the head of the New York City mafia, and other mob leaders who jumped at the chance to take down the Axis powers. *Operation Underworld* was the code name for this historic partnership between the United States military and the Italian mafia. This partnership became an important key in winning the Second World War. For one moment, patriotism brought together bitter enemies who unified under a common goal.

Entering the Promised Land

Our understanding of spiritual warfare has shifted as we have gone through this book together. God has been restoring our fighting spirit, and He has uncovered the revelation that we have been armed for victory. Now is the time to advance. This is the moment when God calls us to pursue, overtake, and recover all that the enemy has stolen from us (see 1 Sam. 30:8). It's time to possess the awakening.

There's one final weapon we need as we take up spiritual arms against the enemy and possess the Promised Land of revival. We must learn to work side by side with dramatically different people who are all marching toward the same goal.

I'm not at all suggesting that the church should partner with the criminal underworld in order to advance God's Kingdom, though I do believe that God will rally the unsaved to support the church in this final revival. After all, a free and blessed nation benefits saint and sinner alike (see Matt. 5:45).

What I am suggesting is that if two forces as drastically different as the mafia and the military can come together because of the urgency of the hour, *the different camps within the church ought to be able to do the same.*

The hour we find ourselves in is no less urgent—and time is running out. We can no longer allow the different factions within the church to sit in their separate corners and wag their fingers at one another. We must unify or die.

After the death of Joshua, the children of Israel were divided and dismayed. They had *entered* the Promised Land, but now they needed to *possess* the land. This was the situation in the opening chapter of the book of Judges:

> *Now after the death of Joshua it came to pass, that the children of Israel asked the Lord, saying, Who shall go up for us against the Canaanites first, to fight against them?* (Judges 1:1)

Here is the lesson: just because we're *in* doesn't mean that we *win*. God intentionally left enemies in the Promised Land. This shows us that the Promised Land is not a representation of Heaven. There are no enemies in Heaven. The Promised Land is a picture of the promises that God has given to us in Christ. It is true that we get access into this land when we're saved, but victory is not automatic. God has left some enemies for us to contend with. Why? Judges 3 gives us the answer:

Now these are the nations which the Lord left, to prove Israel by them, even as many of Israel as had not known all the wars of Canaan; only that the generations of the children of Israel might know, to teach them war, at the least such as before knew nothing thereof (Judges 3:1-2).

A generation had emerged that didn't know anything about the struggle it had taken to get to the Promised Land. They weren't learning from the examples of their forefathers, and they were unarmed for the battles ahead. Joshua and Caleb were the only ones left who remembered the struggle. And now, at 110 years of age, Joshua was dead.

These generals understood from their trials in the wilderness that before you could conquer the enemy, you had to conquer yourself. If you can't win the victory over the inward enemies of selfish desires, impatience, and carnality, you will never be able to defeat your outward adversaries.

We have too many in the church today who are attempting to cast out devils but can't control their own flesh. It's a recipe for disaster. Jesus talked about this with His disciples:

Then said Jesus unto his disciples, If any man will come after me, let him deny himself, and take up his cross, and follow me. For whosoever will save his life shall lose it: and whosoever will lose his life for my sake shall find it. For what is a man profited, if he shall gain the whole world, and lose his own soul? or what shall a man give in exchange for his soul? (Matthew 16:24-26)

How do we crucify our flesh? The cross is an interesting means of humiliation and execution in that we cannot crucify ourselves. Spiritually speaking, we may be able to nail our feet and maybe one hand, but if we're going to get that other hand nailed up there, we're going to need some help. God uses relationships to humble us. We need one another.

> *A new commandment I give unto you, That ye love one another; as I have loved you, that ye also love one another. By this shall all men know that ye are my disciples, if ye have love one to another* (John 13:34-35).

We must yield to this holy humility that creates supernatural unity. This is where the power is. Many Christians like to claim that they have the power to bind and loose the enemy, but they've taken that verse out of context. Neither Matthew 16:19 nor Matthew 18:18 are promises for individuals. The power to bind and loose is given to a *unified church*. We can't walk in this kind of authority on our own.

Simeon and Judah

The Tribe of Judah understood this, so they looked to partner with a different camp in order to possess the land:

> *And the Lord said, Judah shall go up: behold, I have delivered the land into his hand. And Judah said unto Simeon his brother, Come up with me into my lot, that we may fight against the Canaanites; and I likewise will go with thee into thy lot. So Simeon went with him* (Judges 1:2-3).

Man tends toward tribalism. We naturally seek the safety of the echo chamber where we can have our own ideas parroted back. The nation of Israel had been divided into twelve tribes. Instead of walking in unity, they often despised one another. Yet we see these two camps coming together to possess the land.

In much the same way, I believe that God is bringing the camps together in these last days. What we see prophetically pictured in this historical account is happening before our very eyes today.

The Hebrew name for *Judah* speaks of prophetic praise. Its root meaning references the throwing of sound from the mouth like a ball from a hand. The name *Simeon* means "to hear." These are two very different tribes. One's focus is on *hearing* while the other's is on *declaring*. When they come together, their focus is on *conquering*. There are two camps in the Body of Christ that fit this characterization today.

There are many different tribes in today's church, and yet we somehow always lean toward one ditch or the other. One tribe generally tends to be super-spiritual; the other is apt to be super-scriptural.

The hyper-spiritual saint is so open to error and false doctrine that they are in danger of *hellfire*, while the hyper-theological saint is so bound by legalism that they are in danger of *no fire*. The spiritually goofy are so worried about quenching the Spirit that they're open to anything, while the religious prudes of our day are so worried about error that they won't allow anything.

When we go to the Word of God, we see that both are wrong. The Kingdom of God is not Judah *or* Simeon; it is

Judah *and* Simeon—speaking and hearing coming together to accomplish one purpose.

Those who lean toward the prophetic may look down their noses at believers they think are too legalistic and old-fashioned in their Word of Faith roots. At the same time, those who have been taught well in the Word might decry the perceived shallowness of the prophetic camp.

I believe that both are key to the next great revival. Judah and Simeon must come together if we wish to possess this awakening.

In Judges 1:3, it took praise to awaken the ear. We know that faith comes by hearing and hearing by the Word of God (see Rom. 10:17). Today, the ear of the Word of Faith movement is in danger of entering a feedback loop, while the mouth of the prophecy camp could end up with no one but themselves to prophesy to.

Think what could happen when the ear and the mouth work together. World-changing faith will be birthed within the Body! I've placed in the appendix a powerful vision by Tommy Hicks that perfectly illustrates what can happen when we come together as one body.

We have to ask ourselves: are we capable of partnering with a different tribe? It's not easy. They don't worship like we do. They haven't matured in the same areas we have—but the reverse is also true. They may talk differently and focus on things we feel are of secondary importance.

But instead of looking at these differences as a reason to separate ourselves, we should be looking at them as the reason to unite. We are strong in one area; they are strong in another—that's why we need each other. Think what we could accomplish together!

From my unique perspective, I am beginning to see these differing camps come together around a fascination with the end times. We're not truly armed until we have this kind of partnership. Agreement unlocks the arsenal of God.

The Tumor Just Fell Off!

When I was the director of an international prayer center, I had the privilege of praying with thousands of people. Most of these I don't remember, but there are a few that I will never forget.

One day in particular, we were slammed. The phone lines were ringing off the hook, we were understaffed, and the administrative side of things had piled up. I was swamped, and I wasn't feeling particularly spiritual. That was when a precious woman walked into our offices asking for prayer.

She had a cancerous growth on her body the size of a tangerine. I remember that she was wearing a sweatshirt because any other clothing was painful when it rubbed against this growth. In the swirl of the moment, my heart sank because I felt completely unarmed. I didn't think that I had what I needed to fight this battle.

Some of you may be facing similar situations. What do you do when you're faced with a situation that's like a gut punch—and you are totally unprepared for it?

I quickly called in one of my key staff members, and we began to pray and worship in the Spirit. As we stood in agreement, the presence of God showed up in that room and a Bible verse that I didn't know I knew jumped up in my spirit:

Every plant, which my heavenly Father hath not planted, shall be rooted up (Matthew 15:13).

I said, "Cancer, you were not planted there by God. Therefore, you have no right to remain in her body. I curse you, and I command you to be rooted up, in Jesus' Name!" The power of God hit that room and she knew that she had been healed in that moment. She went into the restroom to remove the bandage. When she pulled away the dressing, she discovered that the tumor had fallen off! She had received a miracle. But how?

As we militantly worshiped and prayed in the Spirit, a portal was opened through which God could give us prophetic intelligence. When He spoke that verse to us, we got on a war footing and entered into command praying. All of this came together—and was only possible—through our partnership in prayer. People from very different camps and dramatically different backgrounds came together, and the miraculous was released.

Agreement unlocks the arsenal of God. Throughout history, desperation has brought people together across racial, cultural, and spiritual lines. We must find the strength to step out of the comfort of our own camps and rouse this sleeping giant called the church before it's too late. Only then will we be truly armed for victory.

Epilogue

The activation of our spiritual armament occurs on many levels. From a simple nudge in our spirits to pray a certain way about a situation, to the operation of the gifts of the Spirit, to a full-blown prayer meeting with hundreds gathered in militant worship, God is arming His people to pray.

Two things happen in natural warfare; the same two things happen in spiritual warfare. A natural army fights not only to take back enemy-held territory, but to advance into new territory they have not yet conquered.

The same thing is true on the spiritual front. We can—and must—take back what the enemy has stolen from us. We can—and must—take back our healing, our relationships, our finances, our families, and our futures. We must take back everything the enemy has taken from us. This is accomplished through prayer, armed with the supernatural end-time prayer strategies that God has revealed to us.

However, that is not the end of the story! Even if we have already encountered and moved in every method of prayer discussed in this book, we still have more to learn. One of the most amazing things about the Word of God is that it is a book of continual, ongoing revelation. The more we know, the more we realize there is to know!

This side of glory, we will never know it all. There will always be revelation to reach for, divine intelligence to uncover, and prophetic mysteries to be revealed. Even the works of Jesus Himself on the earth are spoken of as being so numerous that you would lose count trying to tabulate them:

And there are also many other things which Jesus did, the which, if they should be written every one, I suppose that even the world itself could not contain the books that should be written. Amen (John 21:25).

We are called to not only take back enemy-held territory, but we are also called to advance the Kingdom of God. We are called to step out into uncharted waters. We are called to press forward into new frontiers. We are called to press toward the mark and take new ground in the Spirit.

How much more will we, in the dispensation of the church, experience the power of God displayed in our lives as we serve Him? How much more will God be glorified by the works we do, empowered by the Holy Spirit? How many books will be written about the marvelous acts of the church in the end times?

Trained and equipped with prayer strategies from the halls of Heaven, the most glorious days of the church are just ahead! We are truly armed for victory!

TOMMY HICKS' VISION

Tommy Hicks was an American healing revivalist who rose to fame in the Argentinian revivals of 1954. He secured a meeting with President Juan Perón to ask permission to hold a salvation and healing crusade in the country. After requesting and receiving prayer, Perón himself was healed of a long-standing skin condition. This prompted him to give Tommy Hicks access to the largest stadium in the country, where overflowing crowds came and received ministry. Over a two-month period, 3 million people attended his meetings, with 300,000 decisions for Christ and many, many healings reported.

This attracted the attention of the Full Gospel Business Men's Fellowship, which became a large financial backer for his revival meetings.

In 1961, he received a prophetic vision of the end

*times, which has been recounted many times. By per-
mission, that vision is recorded here to inspire your
faith and encourage you in your walk with God.*

When this vision appeared to me, I suddenly found myself
at a great height. I was looking down upon the earth, when suddenly the whole world came into view—every nation, every kin-
dred, every tongue came before my sight. From the east and
the west; from the north and the south; I recognized the countries and cities that I had been in. I was almost in fear and trem-
bling as I stood beholding the great sight before me. At that
moment, when the world came into view, it began to lightning
and thunder.

As the lightning flashed over the face of the earth, my eyes
went downward and I was facing the north. Suddenly I beheld
what looked like a great giant. As I stared and looked at it, I was
almost bewildered by the sight. The giant was gigantic. His feet
seemed to reach to the North Pole and his head to the South
Pole. His arms were stretched from sea to sea. I could not even
begin to understand whether this was a mountain or whether
this was a giant. As I watched, I suddenly beheld that it was a
great giant. I could see he was struggling for life, to even live. His
body was covered with debris from head to foot; and at times
this great giant would move his body and act as though he would
rise up. When he did, thousands of little creatures seemed to run
away. Hideous looking creatures would run away from this giant
and when he would become calm, they would come back.

All of a sudden this great giant lifted one hand toward the
heavens, and then he lifted his other hand. When he did, these

creatures by the thousands seemed to flee away from this giant and go out into the night. Slowly this great giant began to rise and as he did, his head and hands went into the clouds. As he arose to his feet he seemed to have cleansed himself from the debris and filth that was upon him and he began to raise his hands into the heavens as though praising the Lord. As he raised his hands, they went even unto the clouds.

Suddenly, every cloud became silver, the most beautiful silver that I have ever known. As I watched the phenomenon, it was so great, I could not even begin to understand what it all meant, I was so stirred as I watched it. I cried unto the Lord and I said, "Oh, Lord, what is the meaning of this?" And it felt as if I was actually in the Spirit and I could feel the presence of the Lord, even as I was asleep. From those clouds, suddenly there came great drops of liquid light raining down upon this mighty giant. Slowly, slowly, this giant began to melt—began to sink, as it were, into the very earth itself. As he melted, his whole form seemed to have melted upon the face of the earth. This great rain began to come down. Liquid drops of light began to flood the very earth itself. As I watched this giant that seemed to melt, suddenly it became millions of people over the face of the earth. As I beheld the giant before me, people stood up all over the world. They were lifting their hands and they were praising the Lord.

At that very moment there came a great thunder that seemed to roar from the heavens. I turned my eyes toward the heavens, and suddenly I saw a figure glistening in white, but somehow I knew that it was the Lord Jesus Christ. HE stretched forth His hand. As He did, He would stretch it forth to one, and to another, and to another as He stretched forth His hand upon the peoples and the nations of the world—men and women. As He pointed toward them, this liquid light seemed to flow from His hand into this person and a mighty anointing of God came upon them. Those people began to go forth in the name of the Lord. I do not know how long I watched it. It seemed it went into days and weeks and months. I beheld this Christ as He continued to stretch forth His hand. But there was a tragedy. There were many people, as He stretched forth His hands that refused the anointing of God and call of God. I saw men and women that I knew, people that I felt that certainly they would receive the call of God. As He stretched forth His hand toward this one, and towards that one, they simply bowed their heads and began to back away. To each of those that seemed to bow down and back away, they seemed to go into darkness. Blackness seemed to swallow them everywhere.

I was bewildered as I watched it. These people that He had anointed covered the earth. There were hundreds of thousands of these people all over the world—in Africa, Asia, Russia, China, America—all over the world. The anointing of God was upon these people as they went forth in the name of the Lord. I saw these men and women as they went forth. They were ditch diggers, they were washer women, they were rich men, they were poor men. I saw people who were bound with paralysis and sickness, and blindness and deafness. As the Lord stretched forth His hand to give them this anointing, they became well, they became healed—and they went forth.

This is the miracle of it. This is the glorious miracle of it. Those people would stretch forth their hands exactly as the Lord did, and it seemed that there was this same liquid fire that seemed to be in their hands. As they stretched forth their hands, they said, "According to my word, be thou made whole." As these people continued in this mighty end-time ministry, I did not fully realize what it was. I looked to the Lord and said, "What is the meaning of this?" He said, "This is that, that I will do in the last day. I will restore all the cankerworm, the palmerworm, the caterpillar—I will restore all that they have destroyed. This My people in the end-time, shall go forth and as a mighty army shall they sweep over the face of the earth."

As I was at this great height, I could behold the whole world. I watched these people as they were going to and fro over the face of the earth. Suddenly there was a man in Africa, and in a moment he was transported in the Spirit of God, and perhaps he was in Russia, or China, or America, or some other place, and vice versa. All over the world these people went. They came through fire and through pestilence and through famine. Neither fire nor persecution—nothing seemed to stop them. Angry mobs came to them with swords and with guns, and like Jesus, they passed through the multitude and they could not find them. But they went forth in the name of the Lord. Everywhere they stretched forth their hands, the sick were healed, the blind eyes were opened. There was not a long prayer. I never saw a church, and I never saw or heard a denomination. These people were going in the name of the Lord of Hosts.

As they marched forward as the ministry of Christ in the end-time, these people ministered to the multitudes over the face of the earth. Tens of thousands, even millions seemed to come to the Lord Jesus Christ as these people stood forth and gave the message of the kingdom—of the coming kingdom in this last hour. It was so glorious! It seemed there were those that rebelled. They would become angry. They tried to attack those workers who were giving the message. God is going to give to the world a demonstration in this last hour such as the world has never known. These men and women are of all walks of life. Degrees will mean nothing. I saw these workers as they were going over the face of the earth. When one would seem to stumble and fall, another would come and pick him up. There were no big "I" little "you." Every mountain was brought low and every valley was exalted, and they seemed to have one thing in common—there was a divine love that seemed to flow forth from these people as they went together, as they worked together, as they lived together. It was the theme of their life. They continued and it seemed the days went by as I stood and beheld this sight. I could only cry—and sometimes I laughed.

It was so wonderful as these people went throughout the face of the whole earth showing forth God's power in this last end-time. As I watched from the very heaven itself, there were times when great deluges of this liquid light seemed to fall upon great congregations. The congregations would lift their hands and seemingly praise God for hours and even days, as the Spirit of God came upon them. God said, "I will pour out My Spirit upon all flesh." That is exactly the thing that God was doing.

From every man and woman that received this power and the anointing of God, the miracles of God flowed continuously.

Suddenly there was another great clap of thunder that seemed to resound around the world. Again I heard the voice saying: "Now, this is My people; this is My beloved bride." When the voice spoke, I looked upon the earth and I could see the lakes and the mountains. The graves were opened and people from all over the world, the saints of all ages, seemed to be rising. As they rose from the graves, suddenly all these people came from every direction, from the east and the west, from the north and the south, and they seemed to be forming again this gigantic body. As the dead in Christ seemed to be rising first, I could hardly comprehend it.

It was so marvelous. It was so far beyond anything I could ever dream or think of. This huge body suddenly began to form and take shape again, and its shape was in the form of the mighty giant, but this time it was different. It was arrayed in the most beautiful, gorgeous white. Its garments were without spot or wrinkle as this body began to form, and the people of all ages seemed to be gathering into this body. Slowly, from the heavens above, the Lord Jesus came and became the head. I heard another clap of thunder that said, "This is My beloved bride for whom I have waited. She will come forth, even tried by fire. This is she that I have loved from the beginning of time." As I watched, my eyes turned to the far north and I saw great destruction, men and women in anguish and crying out, and buildings destroyed. Then I heard again, the fourth voice that said, "Now My wrath being poured out upon the face of the earth."

From the ends of the whole world, it seemed that there were great vials of God's wrath being poured out upon the face of the earth. I can remember it as I beheld the awful sight of seeing cities, and whole nations going down into destruction. I could hear the weeping and the wailing. I could hear people crying. They seemed to cry as they went into caves, but the caves and the mountains opened up. They leaped in water, but the water would not drown them. There was nothing that seemingly could destroy them. They wanted to take their lives but they did not succeed.

Again I turned my eyes toward the glorious sight of this body arrayed in the beautiful white shining garment. Slowly, slowly, it began to lift from the earth, and as it did, I awoke. This sight that I had beheld—I had seen the end-of-time ministry, the last hour. Again on July 27 at 2:30 in the morning the same revelation, the same vision, came again exactly as it did before. My life has been changed as I realize that we are living in that end time, for all over the world God is anointing men and women with this ministry. It will not be doctrine. It will not be "churchianity," but it is going to be Jesus Christ. They will give forth the word of the Lord and are going to say, I heard it so many times in the vision, "According to my word, it shall be done." Oh people, listen to me! "According to my word, it shall be done." We are going to be clothed with power and anointing from God. We won't have to preach sermons. We won't have to depend on man, nor will we be denominational echoes, but we will have the power of the living God! We will fear no man, but will go in the name of the Lord of Hosts![1]

Note

1. Electronic Copyright © 2009 Tony Cauchi, www
   .revival-library.org, reprinted by permission.

ABOUT ALAN DIDIO

After experiencing a radical spiritual encounter at the age of seventeen, Alan DiDio was born again, instantly transforming him from a dogmatic atheist to a passionate follower of Jesus. Taught in a Word-based church, he learned early on how to stand in faith. Not long after giving his life to Christ, Pastor Alan went off to Bible college and continued serving with a national ministry for twelve years and working on staff for nearly seven. In that time, he gained experience in every possible area of ministry from running an international prayer center to traveling across the country spreading the Gospel.

Since then, he's founded Encounter Christ Church in his hometown and taken the Gospel to nations such as Pakistan, China, Israel, Haiti, and Guatemala. He also hosts the *Encounter Underground* podcast and *Encounter Today* on YouTube, which reaches tens of thousands of people around the world with the Gospel of Jesus Christ.

Pastor Alan and his wife, Tera, have two children and consider family to be the most important ministry any believer is called to.